D0966648

THE TURNER THESIS
CONCERNING THE ROLE OF THE
FRONTIER IN AMERICAN HISTORY

Revised Edition

Problems in American Civilization

UNDER THE EDITORIAL DIRECTION OF *George Rogers Taylor*

The Turner Thesis

CONCERNING THE ROLE OF THE FRONTIER IN AMERICAN HISTORY

Revised Edition

EDITED WITH AN INTRODUCTION BY

George Rogers Taylor

Problems in American Civilization

D. C. HEATH AND COMPANY: Boston

INTRODUCTION

BY the close of the nineteenth century the United States had become a major world power, and now at the middle of the twentieth century this country has achieved a position of world leadership. Today no great nation can compare with us in economic productivity and living standards; only Russia rivals us in military power. Yet despite our development into an industrial and political colossus, we maintain in most of our customs and institutions a republican form of government and a democratic spirit. How have we been able to do this? What are the factors which have shaped our growth and molded our character? Where shall we look for a meaningful explanation of our history?

Theories designed to interpret historical development, though they deal with the past, are significant chiefly in helping us to understand the problems of the present and the future. This is why in every age a nation needs to rewrite its history. Today international questions loom large and there is a strong tendency to condemn what is regarded as the narrow nationalism of the past. Yet the role which the United States plays on the world stage today and will play tomorrow, the policies which we adopt and the contributions which we bring to world councils, will be determined in no small part by our understanding and interpretation of our own past. It is for this reason that the controversy over the Turner thesis is important.

Writing during the last decade of the nineteenth century and the first three decades of the twentieth century, Frederick Jackson Turner developed a new approach to American history, an interpretation which has come to be known as the frontier hypothesis or the Turner thesis. Earlier American historians had written mainly from the point of view of the eastern seaboard. Their emphasis had been on European influences and colonial origins. Constitutional issues, especially those which arose between the North and the South and culminated in the Civil War, had claimed major attention. Turner sought a fresh point of view, a more meaningful approach to an understanding of the new America which had become continental in extent and whose frontier was, after nearly three hundred years, finally being closed.

As to what the frontier thesis is, we can well afford to let Turner speak for himself in the first two readings in this volume, which contain the gist of his new approach. The first essay, "The Significance of the Frontier in American History," was read before the American Historical Association in Chicago in 1893. Though he was only thirty-two years old and recently out of graduate school, Turner in this paper, which has become the most widely known essay in American history, revolutionized historical thought in the United States. To the theme of this early address he recurred again and again in later writings, often stressing in particular the role which the frontier had played in stimulating the growth of democracy in this country. One of his best-known works with this emphasis is an essay written in 1903 entitled "Contributions of the West to American Democracy." It appears as the second item in the present volume.

In the thirty years following Turner's announcement of his brilliant thesis of 1893 the whole center of gravity of American historical writing and teaching shifted. Almost overnight his ideas captured the imagination of American historians and set them, for a generation, to studying the frontier and interpreting American development in relation to the opening of the West. The number of his disciples was increased by his extraordinary personal influence as a teacher of history at Wisconsin and Harvard, mentioned in several of the selections in this volume. A student of Turner's and one of the leading historical scholars of the time, Carl Becker, has this to say of him:

Three qualities of the man's mind made upon me a profound and indelible impression. These qualities were: a lively and irrepressible intellectual curiosity; a refreshing freedom from personal preoccupations and didactic motives; a quite unusual ability to look out upon the wide world in a humane and friendly way, with a vision unobscured by academic inhibitions. These are also the qualities, I think, which have enabled him to make an "original contribution" (not so common a performance as is often supposed) to the study of American history.[1]

The Turner thesis reigned almost unchallenged during the first quarter of the 20th century. Then a growing revolt

spread as one scholar after another trained his heaviest guns on various aspects of the frontier hypothesis. The readings provide a sampling of the chief criticisms which have been raised. In the third selection Benjamin F. Wright, Jr., formerly Professor of Government at Harvard University and now President of Smith College, directs his attack primarily against Turner's view of the frontier as a democratizing influence in our history. The fourth essay illustrates the attack on Turner by those who rebuke him for what he does not do, for his failure, as they believe, to see the significance of such forces as urbanization, the industrial revolution, and the rise and importance of "basic class antagonisms." One of the most vigorous of these critics, Professor Louis M. Hacker of Columbia University, here condemns Turner for his neglect of certain economic factors which he believes worthy of major emphasis. In the fifth essay, Professor George Wilson Pierson of Yale University subjects the frontier hypothesis to a general re-examination and overhauling. In the last of the selections from Turner's critics, Professor Carlton J. H. Hayes of Columbia University ascribes the intellectual isolationism of this country in part at least to the influence of the frontier hypothesis.

During the 1930's and 40's the tide ran strongly against the frontier hypothesis. One of the few scholars who answered the critics was Avery Craven who was a student of Turner at Harvard and later Professor of History at the University of Chicago. His essay is the first of a group of three selections which conclude the readings in this volume and present a more favorable view of the Turner Thesis. The last two selections are relatively recent contributions which some believe reflect an ebbing of the anti-Turnerian

---

[1] "Frederick Jackson Turner" in *American Masters of Social Science*, Howard W. Odum, ed. (New York, 1927), p. 295. This quotation is reproduced by permission of Henry Holt and Company, Inc.

tide. In the eighth selection Walter Prescott Webb, Professor of History at the University of Texas, develops and widens the frontier concept. The final item is by two Columbia University scholars, Stanley Elkins and Eric McKetrick. They offer a positive and novel reply to those who have questioned Turner's emphasis on the democratic influence of the frontier.

What is the upshot of all this controversy? Must Turner's frontier thesis now be abandoned as a useless, perhaps even a dangerous, hypothesis? Or does Turner's work still stand in its essentials despite the savage attacks which have been made upon it since the 1920's. This is the problem presented by the readings in this volume.

Some honestly believe that the last word has been spoken, that the frontier hypothesis is now as dead as the dodo. Others remain unimpressed by the sound and fury of the attack, holding that, though clarification is desirable and some amendments should be made, the Turner thesis provides today a sound and useful approach for those who seek to understand our past in order better to meet the problems of the present.

CONTENTS

THE CLASH OF ISSUES

The thesis:

"The existence of an area of free land, its continuous recession, and the advance of American settlement westward, explain American development."

"The true point of view in the history of this nation is not the Atlantic coast, it is the Great West."

— FREDERICK JACKSON TURNER

A statement by a leading disciple of Turner:

"The frontier hypothesis presents the most attractive single explanation of the distinctive trends of American history."

— FREDERIC L. PAXSON

But the critics say:

"Only by a study of the origins and growth of American capitalism and imperialism can we obtain insight into the nature and complexity of the problems confronting us today. And I am prepared to submit that perhaps the chief reason for the absence of this proper understanding was the futile hunt for a unique 'American spirit' which Frederick Jackson Turner began forty years ago and in which he involved most of America's historical scholars from that time until now."

— LOUIS M. HACKER

"In what it proposes, the frontier hypothesis needs painstaking revision. By what it fails to mention, the theory today disqualifies itself as an adequate guide to American development."

— GEORGE WILSON PIERSON

Frederick Jackson Turner:

THE SIGNIFICANCE OF THE FRONTIER IN AMERICAN HISTORY

IN a recent bulletin of the Superintendent of the Census for 1890 appear these significant words: "Up to and including 1880 the country had a frontier of settlement, but at present the unsettled area has been so broken into by isolated bodies of settlement that there can hardly be said to be a frontier line. In the discussion of its extent, its westward movement, etc., it can not, therefore, any longer have a place in the census reports." This brief official statement marks the closing of a great historic movement. Up to our own day American history has been in a large degree the history of the colonization of the Great West. The existence of an area of free land, its continuous recession, and the advance of American settlement westward, explain American development.

Behind institutions, behind constitutional forms and modifications, lie the vital forces that call these organs into life and shape them to meet changing conditions. The peculiarity of American institutions is the fact that they have been compelled to adapt themselves to the changes of an expanding people — to the changes involved in crossing a continent, in winning a wilderness, and in developing at each area of this progress out of the primitive economic and political conditions of the frontier into the complexity of city life. Said Calhoun in 1817, "We are great, and rapidly — I was about to say fearfully — growing!" So saying, he touched the distinguishing feature of American life. All peoples show development; the germ theory of politics has been sufficiently emphasized. In the case of most nations, however, the development has occurred in a limited area; and if the nation has expanded, it has met other growing peoples whom it has conquered. But in the case of the United States we have a different phenomenon. Limiting our attention to the Atlantic coast, we have the familiar phenomenon of the evolution of institutions in a limited area, such as the rise of representative government; the differentiation of simple colonial governments into complex organs; the progress from primitive industrial society, without division of labor, up to manufacturing civilization. But we have in addition to this a recurrence of the process of evolution in each western area reached in the process of expansion. Thus American development has exhibited not merely advance along a single line, but a return to primitive conditions on a continually advancing frontier line, and a new development for that area. American social

From *The Frontier in American History* by Frederick Jackson Turner, copyright 1920 by Frederick Jackson Turner, copyright 1948 by Caroline M. S. Turner. Reprinted by permission of Henry Holt and Company, Inc.

development has been continually beginning over again on the frontier. This perennial rebirth, this fluidity of American life, this expansion westward with its new opportunities, its continuous touch with the simplicity of primitive society, furnish the forces dominating American character. The true point of view in the history of this nation is not the Atlantic coast, it is the Great West. Even the slavery struggle, which is made so exclusive an object of attention by writers like Professor von Holst, occupies its important place in American history because of its relation to westward expansion.

In this advance, the frontier is the outer edge of the wave — the meeting point between savagery and civilization. Much has been written about the frontier from the point of view of border warfare and the chase, but as a field for the serious study of the economist and the historian it has been neglected.

The American frontier is sharply distinguished from the European frontier — a fortified boundary line running through dense populations. The most significant thing about the American frontier is, that it lies at the hither edge of free land. In the census reports it is treated as the margin of that settlement which has a density of two or more to the square mile. The term is an elastic one, and for our purposes does not need sharp definition. We shall consider the whole frontier belt, including the Indian country and the outer margin of the "settled area" of the census reports. This paper will make no attempt to treat the subject exhaustively; its aim is simply to call attention to the frontier as a fertile field for investigation, and to suggest some of the problems which arise in connection with it.

In the settlement of America we have to observe how European life entered the continent, and how America modified and developed that life and reacted on Europe. Our early history is the study of European germs developing in an American environment. Too exclusive attention has been paid by institutional students to the Germanic origins, too little to the American factors. The frontier is the line of most rapid and effective Americanization. The wilderness masters the colonist. It finds him a European in dress, industries, tools, modes of travel, and thought. It takes him from the railroad car and puts him in the birch canoe. It strips off the garments of civilization and arrays him in the hunting shirt and the moccasin. It puts him in the log cabin of the Cherokee and Iroquois and runs an Indian palisade around him. Before long he has gone to planting Indian corn and plowing with a sharp stick; he shouts the war cry and takes the scalp in orthodox Indian fashion. In short, at the frontier the environment is at first too strong for the man. He must accept the conditions which it furnishes, or perish, and so he fits himself into the Indian clearings and follows the Indian trails. Little by little he transforms the wilderness, but the outcome is not the old Europe, not simply the development of Germanic germs, any more than the first phenomenon was a case of reversion to the Germanic mark. The fact is, that here is a new product that is American. At first, the frontier was the Atlantic coast. It was the frontier of Europe in a very real sense. Moving westward, the frontier became more and more American. As successive terminal moraines result from successive glaciations, so each frontier leaves its traces behind it, and when it becomes a settled area the region still partakes of the frontier characteristics. Thus the advance of the frontier has meant a steady movement away from the influence of

Europe, a steady growth of independence on American lines. And to study this advance, the men who grew up under these conditions, and the political, economic, and social results of it, is to study the really American part of our history.

In the course of the seventeenth century the frontier was advanced up the Atlantic river courses, just beyond the "fall line," and the tidewater region became the settled area. In the first half of the eighteenth century another advance occurred. Traders followed the Delaware and Shawnee Indians to the Ohio as early as the end of the first quarter of the century. Gov. Spotswood, of Virginia, made an expedition in 1714 across the Blue Ridge. The end of the first quarter of the century saw the advance of the Scotch-Irish and the Palatine Germans up the Shenandoah Valley into the western part of Virginia, and along the Piedmont region of the Carolinas. The Germans in New York pushed the frontier of settlement up the Mohawk to German Flats. In Pennsylvania the town of Bedford indicates the line of settlement. Settlements had begun on New River, a branch of the Kanawha, and on the sources of the Yadkin and French Broad. The King attempted to arrest the advance by his proclamation of 1763, forbidding settlements beyond the sources of the rivers flowing into the Atlantic; but in vain. In the period of the Revolution the frontier crossed the Alleghenies into Kentucky and Tennessee, and the upper waters of the Ohio were settled. When the first census was taken in 1790, the continuous settled area was bounded by a line which ran near the coast of Maine, and included New England except a portion of Vermont and New Hampshire, New York along the Hudson and up the Mohawk about Schenectady, eastern and southern Pennsylvania, Virginia well across the Shenandoah Valley, and the Carolinas and eastern Georgia. Beyond this region of continuous settlement were the small settled areas of Kentucky and Tennessee, and the Ohio, with the mountains intervening between them and the Atlantic area, thus giving a new and important character to the frontier. The isolation of the region increased its peculiarly American tendencies, and the need of transportation facilities to connect it with the East called out important schemes of internal improvement, which will be noted farther on. The "West," as a self-conscious section, began to evolve.

From decade to decade distinct advances of the frontier occurred. By the census of 1820 the settled area included Ohio, southern Indiana and Illinois, southeastern Missouri, and about one-half of Louisiana. This settled area had surrounded Indian areas, and the management of these tribes became an object of political concern. The frontier region of the time lay along the Great Lakes, where Astor's American Fur Company operated in the Indian trade, and beyond the Mississippi, where Indian traders extended their activity even to the Rocky Mountains; Florida also furnished frontier conditions. The Mississippi River region was the scene of typical frontier settlements.

The rising steam navigation on western waters, the opening of the Erie Canal, and the westward extension of cotton culture added five frontier states to the Union in this period. Grund, writing in 1836, declares: "It appears then that the universal disposition of Americans to emigrate to the western wilderness, in order to enlarge their dominion over inanimate nature, is the actual result of an expansive power which is inherent in them, and which by continually agitating all classes of society is constantly throwing a large portion of the whole population on the extreme confines of the State, in order to gain space for its development. Hardly is a new State or Territory formed before the same principle manifests itself again and gives rise to a further emigration; and so is it destined to go on until a physical barrier must finally obstruct its progress."

In the middle of this century the line indicated by the present eastern boundary of Indian Territory, Nebraska, and Kansas marked the frontier of the Indian country. Minnesota and Wisconsin still exhibited frontier conditions, but the distinctive frontier of the period is found in California, where the gold discoveries had sent a sudden tide of adventurous miners, and in Oregon, and the settlements in Utah. As the frontier had leaped over the Alleghenies, so now it skipped the Great Plains and the Rocky Mountains; and in the same way that the advance of the frontiersmen beyond the Alleghenies had caused the rise of important questions of transportation and internal improvement, so now the settlers beyond the Rocky Mountains needed means of communication with the East, and in the furnishing of these arose the settlement of the Great Plains and the development of still another kind of frontier life. Railroads, fostered by land grants, sent an increasing tide of immigrants into the Far West. The United States Army fought a series of Indian wars in Minnesota, Dakota, and the Indian Territory.

By 1880 the settled area had been pushed into northern Michigan, Wisconsin, and Minnesota, along Dakota rivers, and in the Black Hills region, and was ascending the rivers of Kansas and Nebraska. The development of mines in Colorado had drawn isolated frontier settlements into that region, and Montana and Idaho were receiving settlers. The frontier was found in these mining camps and the ranches of the Great Plains. The superintendent of the census for 1890 reports, as previously stated, that the settlements of the West lie so scattered over the region that there can no longer be said to be a frontier line.

In these successive frontiers we find natural boundary lines which have served to mark and to affect the characteristics of the frontiers, namely: the "fall line"; the Allegheny Mountains; the Mississippi; the Missouri where its direction approximates north and south; the line of the arid lands, approximately the ninety-ninth meridian; and the Rocky Mountains. The fall line marked the frontier of the seventeenth century; the Alleghenies that of the eighteenth; the Mississippi that of the first quarter of the nineteenth; the Missouri that of the middle of this century (omitting the California movement); and the belt of the Rocky Mountains and the arid tract, the present frontier. Each was won by a series of Indian wars.

At the Atlantic frontier one can study the germs of processes repeated at each successive frontier. We have the complex European life sharply precipitated by the wilderness into the simplicity of primitive conditions. The first frontier had to meet its Indian question, its question of the disposition of the public domain, of the means of intercourse with older settlements, of the extension of political organization, of religious and educational activity. And the settlement of these and similar questions for one frontier served as a guide for the next. The American student needs not to go to the "prim little townships of Sleswick" for illustrations of the law of continuity and development. For example, he may study the origin of our land policies in the colonial land policy; he may see how the system grew by adapting the statutes to the customs of the successive frontiers. He may see how the mining experience in the lead regions of Wisconsin, Illinois, and Iowa was applied to the mining laws of the Sierras, and how our Indian policy has been a series of experimentations on successive frontiers. Each tier of new States has found in the older ones material for its constitutions. Each frontier has made similar contributions to American characters, as will be discussed farther on.

But with all these similarities there are essential differences, due to the place element and the time element. It is evident that the farming frontier of the Mississippi Valley presents different conditions from the mining frontier of the Rocky Mountains. The frontier reached by the Pacific Railroad, surveyed into rectangles, guarded by the United States Army, and recruited by the daily immigrant ship, moves forward at a swifter pace and in a different way than the frontier reached by the birch canoe or the pack horse. The geologist traces patiently the shores of ancient seas, maps their areas, and compares the older and the newer. It would be a work worth the historian's labors to mark these various frontiers and in detail compare one with another. Not only would there result a more adequate conception of American development and characteristics, but invaluable additions would be made to the history of society.

Loria, the Italian economist, has urged the study of colonial life as an aid in understanding the stages of European development, affirming that colonial settlement is for economic science what the mountain is for geology, bringing to light primitive stratifications. "America," he says, "has the key to the historical enigma which Europe has sought for centuries in vain, and the land which has no history reveals luminously the course of universal history." There is much truth in this. The United States lies like a huge page in the history of society. Line by line as we read this continental page from West to East we find the record of social evolution. It begins with the Indian and the hunter; it goes on to tell of the disintegration of savagery by the entrance of the trader, the pathfinder of civilization; we read the annals of the pastoral stage in ranch life; the exploitation of the soil by the raising of unrotated crops of corn and wheat in sparsely settled farming communities; the intensive culture of the denser farm settlement; and finally the manufacturing organization with city and factory system. This page is familiar to the student of census statistics, but how little of it has been used by our historians. Particularly in eastern States this page is a palimpsest. What is now a manufacturing State was in an earlier decade an area of intensive farming. Earlier yet it had been a wheat area, and still earlier the "range" had attracted the cattle-herder. Thus Wisconsin, now developing manufacture, is a State with varied agricultural interests. But earlier it was given over to almost exclusive grain-raising, like North Dakota at the present time.

Each of these areas has had an influence in our economic and political history; the evolution of each into a higher stage has worked political transformations. But what constitutional historian has made any adequate attempt to interpret political facts by the light of these social areas and changes?

The Atlantic frontier was compounded of fisherman, fur-trader, miner, cattle-

raiser, and farmer. Excepting the fisherman, each type of industry was on the
march toward the West, impelled by an
irresistible attraction. Each passed in
successive waves across the continent.
Stand at Cumberland Gap and watch the
procession of civilization, marching single
file — the buffalo following the trail to
the salt springs, the Indian, the fur-trader
and hunter, the cattle-raiser, the pioneer
farmer — and the frontier has passed by.
Stand at South Pass in the Rockies a
century later and see the same procession with wider intervals between. The
unequal rate of advance compels us to
distinguish the frontier into the trader's
frontier, the rancher's frontier, or the
miner's frontier, and the farmer's frontier. When the mines and the cowpens
were still near the fall line the traders'
pack trains were tinkling across the
Alleghenies, and the French on the
Great Lakes were fortifying their posts,
alarmed by the British trader's birch
canoe. When the trappers scaled the
Rockies, the farmer was still near the
mouth of the Missouri.

Why was it that the Indian trader
passed so rapidly across the continent?
What effects followed from the trader's
frontier? The trade was coeval with
American discovery. The Norsemen, Ves-
puccius, Verrazani, Hudson, John Smith,
all trafficked for furs. The Plymouth pilgrims settled in Indian cornfields, and
their first return cargo was of beaver and
lumber. The records of the various New
England colonies show how steadily ex-
ploration was carried into the wilderness
by this trade. What is true for New England is, as would be expected, even
plainer for the rest of the colonies. All
along the coast from Maine to Georgia
the Indian trade opened up the river
courses. Steadily the trader passed westward, utilizing the older lines of French

trade. The Ohio, the Great Lakes, the
Mississippi, the Missouri, and the Platte,
the lines of western advance, were as-
cended by traders. They found the
passes in the Rocky Mountains and
guided Lewis and Clark, Frémont, and
Bidwell. The explanation of the rapidity
of this advance is connected with the
effects of the trader on the Indian. The
trading post left the unarmed tribes at
the mercy of those that had purchased
fire-arms — a truth which the Iroquois
Indians wrote in blood, and so the remote and unvisited tribes gave eager
welcome to the trader. "The savages,"
wrote La Salle, "take better care of us
French than of their own children; from
us only can they get guns and goods."
This accounts for the trader's power and
the rapidity of his advance. Thus the disintegrating forces of civilization entered
the wilderness. Every river valley and
Indian trail became a fissure in Indian
society, and so that society became
honeycombed. Long before the pioneer
farmer appeared on the scene, primitive
Indian life had passed away. The farmers
met Indians armed with guns. The trading frontier, while steadily undermining
Indian power by making the tribes ultimately dependent on the whites, yet,
through its sale of guns, gave to the
Indian increased power of resistance to
the farming frontier. French colonization
was dominated by its trading frontier;
English colonization by its farming frontier. There was an antagonism between
the two frontiers as between the two
nations. Said Duquesne to the Iroquois,
"Are you ignorant of the difference between the king of England and the king
of France? Go see the forts that our king
has established and you will see that you
can still hunt under their very walls.
They have been placed for your advantage in places which you frequent. The

English, on the contrary, are no sooner in possession of a place than the game is driven away. The forest falls before them as they advance, and the soil is laid bare so that you can scarce find the wherewithal to erect a shelter for the night."

And yet, in spite of this opposition of the interests of the trader and the farmer, the Indian trade pioneered the way for civilization. The buffalo trail became the Indian trail, and this became the trader's "trace"; the trails widened into roads, and the roads into turnpikes, and these in turn were transformed into railroads. The same origin can be shown for the railroads of the South, the Far West, and the Dominion of Canada. The trading posts reached by these trails were on the sites of Indian villages which had been placed in positions suggested by nature; and these trading posts, situated so as to command the water systems of the country, have grown into such cities as Albany, Pittsburgh, Detroit, Chicago, St. Louis, Council Bluffs, and Kansas City. Thus civilization in America has followed the arteries made by geology, pouring an ever richer tide through them, until at last the slender paths of aboriginal intercourse have been broadened and interwoven into the complex mazes of modern commercial lines; the wilderness has been interpenetrated by lines of civilization growing ever more numerous. It is like the steady growth of a complex nervous system for the originally simple, inert continent. If one would understand why we are to-day one nation, rather than a collection of isolated states, he must study this economic and social consolidation of the country. In this progress from savage conditions lie topics for the evolutionist.

The effect of the Indian frontier as a consolidating agent in our history is important. From the close of the seventeenth century various intercolonial congresses have been called to treat with Indians and establish common measures of defense. Particularism was strongest in colonies with no Indian frontier. This frontier stretched along the western border like a cord of union. The Indian was a common danger, demanding united action. Most celebrated of these conferences was the Albany congress of 1754, called to treat with the Six Nations, and to consider plans of union. Even a cursory reading of the plan proposed by the congress reveals the importance of the frontier. The powers of the general council and the officers were, chiefly, the determination of peace and war with the Indians, the regulation of Indian trade, the purchase of Indian lands, and the creation and government of new settlements as a security against the Indians. It is evident that the unifying tendencies of the Revolutionary period were facilitated by the previous cooperation in the regulation of the frontier. In this connection may be mentioned the importance of the frontier, from that day to this, as a military training school, keeping alive the power of resistance to aggression, and developing the stalwart and rugged qualities of the frontiersman.

It would not be possible in the limits of this paper to trace the other frontiers across the continent. Travelers of the eighteenth century found the "cowpens" among the canebrakes and peavine pastures of the South, and the "cow drivers" took their droves to Charleston, Philadelphia, and New York. Travelers at the close of the War of 1812 met droves of more than a thousand cattle and swine from the interior of Ohio going to Pennsylvania to fatten for the Philadelphia market. The ranges of the Great Plains, with ranch and cowboy and nomadic life, are things of yesterday and of to-day.

The experience of the Carolina cowpens guided the ranchers of Texas. One element favoring the rapid extension of the rancher's frontier is the fact that in a remote country lacking transportation facilities the product must be in small bulk, or must be able to transport itself, and the cattle-raiser could easily drive his product to market. The effect of these great ranches on the subsequent agrarian history of the localities in which they existed should be studied.

The maps of the census reports show an uneven advance of the farmer's frontier, with tongues of settlement pushed forward and with indentations of wilderness. In part this is due to Indian resistance, in part to the location of river valleys and passes, in part to the unequal force of the centers of frontier attraction. Among the important centers of attraction may be mentioned the following: fertile and favorably situated soils, salt springs, mines, and army posts.

The frontier army post, serving to protect the settlers from the Indians, has also acted as a wedge to open the Indian country, and has been a nucleus for settlement. In this connection mention should also be made of the government military and exploring expeditions in determining the lines of settlement. But all the more important expeditions were greatly indebted to the earliest pathmakers, the Indian guides, the traders and trappers, and the French voyageurs, who were inevitable parts of governmental expeditions from the days of Lewis and Clark. Each expedition was an epitome of the previous factors in western advance.

In an interesting monograph, Victor Hehn has traced the effect of salt upon early European development, and has pointed out how it affected the lines of settlement and the form of administra-

tion. A similar study might be made for the salt springs of the United States. The early settlers were tied to the coast by the need of salt, without which they could not preserve their meats or live in comfort. Writing in 1752, Bishop Spangenburg says of a colony for which he was seeking lands in North Carolina, "They will require salt & other necessaries which they can neither manufacture nor raise. Either they must go to Charleston, which is 300 miles distant . . . Or else they must go to Boling's Point in V^a on a branch of the James & is also 300 miles from here . . . Or else they must go down the Roanoke — I know not how many miles — where salt is brought up from the Cape Fear." This may serve as a typical illustration. An annual pilgrimage to the coast for salt thus became essential. Taking flocks or furs and ginseng root, the early settlers sent their pack trains after seeding time each year to the coast. This proved to be an important educational influence, since it was almost the only way in which the pioneer learned what was going on in the East. But when discovery was made of the salt springs of the Kanawha, and the Holston, and Kentucky, and central New York, the West began to be freed from dependence on the coast. It was in part the effect of finding these salt springs that enabled settlement to cross the mountains.

From the time the mountains rose between the pioneer and the seaboard, a new order of Americanism arose. The West and the East began to get out of touch of each other. The settlements from the sea to the mountains kept connection with the rear and had a certain solidarity. But the over-mountain men grew more and more independent. The East took a narrow view of American advance, and nearly lost these men. Kentucky and Tennessee history bears abundant witness to the truth of this statement. The East began to try to hedge and limit westward expansion. Though Webster could declare that there were no Alleghenies in his politics, yet in politics in general they were a very solid factor.

The exploitation of the beasts took hunter and trader to the west, the exploitation of the grasses took the rancher west, and the exploitation of the virgin soil of the river valleys and prairies attracted the farmer. Good soils have been the most continuous attraction to the farmer's frontier. The land hunger of the Virginians drew them down the rivers into Carolina, in early colonial days; the search for soils took the Massachusetts men to Pennsylvania and to New York. As the eastern lands were taken up migration flowed across them to the west. Daniel Boone, the great backwoodsman, who combined the occupations of hunter, trader, cattle-raiser, farmer, and surveyor — learning, probably from the traders, of the fertility of the lands of the upper Yadkin, where the traders were wont to rest as they took their way to the Indians — left his Pennsylvania home with his father, and passed down the Great Valley road to that stream. Learning from a trader of the game and rich pastures of Kentucky, he pioneered the way for the farmers to that region. Thence he passed to the frontier of Missouri, where his settlement was long a landmark on the frontier. Here again he helped to open the way for civilization, finding salt licks, and trails, and land. His son was among the earliest trappers in the passes of the Rocky Mountains, and his party are said to have been the first to camp on the present site of Denver. His grandson, Col. A. J. Boone, of Colorado, was a power among the Indians of the Rocky Mountains, and was appointed an agent by the government. Kit Carson's mother was a Boone. Thus this family epitomizes the backwoodsman's advance across the continent.

The farmer's advance came in a distinct series of waves. In Peck's New Guide to the West, published in Boston in 1837, occurs this suggestive passage:

Generally, in all the western settlements, three classes, like the waves of the ocean, have rolled one after the other. First comes the pioneer, who depends for the subsistence of his family chiefly upon the natural growth of vegetation, called the "range," and the proceeds of hunting. His implements of agriculture are rude, chiefly of his own make, and his efforts directed mainly to a crop of corn and a "truck patch." The last is a rude garden for growing cabbage, beans, corn for roasting ears, cucumbers, and potatoes. A log cabin, and, occasionally, a stable and corn-crib, and a field of a dozen acres, the timber girdled or "deadened," and fenced, are enough for his occupancy. It is quite immaterial whether he ever becomes the owner of the soil. He is the occupant for the time being, pays no rent, and feels as independent as the "lord of the manor." With a horse, cow, and one or two breeders of swine, he strikes into the woods with his family, and becomes the founder of a new county, or perhaps state. He builds his cabin, gathers around him a few other families of similar tastes and habits, and occupies till the range is somewhat subdued, and hunting a little precarious, or, which is more frequently the case, till the neighbors crowd around, roads, bridges, and fields annoy him, and he lacks elbow room. The preemption law enables him to dispose of his cabin and cornfield to the next class of emigrants; and, to employ his own figures, he "breaks for the high timber," "clears out for the New Purchase," or migrates to Arkansas or Texas, to work the same process over.

The next class of emigrants purchase the lands, add field to field, clear out the roads, throw rough bridges over the streams, put up hewn log houses with glass windows and brick or stone chimneys, occasionally plant orchards, build mills, school-houses, court-houses, etc., and exhibit the picture and forms of plain, frugal, civilized life.

Another wave rolls on. The men of capital and enterprise come. The settler is ready to sell out and take the advantage of the rise in property, push farther into the interior and become, himself, a man of capital and enter-prise in turn. The small village rises to a spacious town or city; substantial edifices of brick, extensive fields, orchards, gardens, col-leges, and churches are seen. Broadcloths, silks, leghorns, crapes, and all the refine-ments, luxuries, elegancies, frivolities, and fashions are in vogue. Thus wave after wave is rolling westward; the real Eldorado is still farther on.

A portion of the two first classes remain stationary amidst the general movement, im-prove their habits and condition, and rise in the scale of society.

The writer has traveled much amongst the first class, the real pioneers. He has lived many years in connection with the second grade; and now the third wave is sweeping over large districts of Indiana, Illinois, and Missouri. Migration has become almost a habit in the West. Hundreds of men can be found, not over 50 years of age, who have settled for the fourth, fifth, or sixth time on a new spot. To sell out and remove only a few hundred miles makes up a portion of the variety of backwoods life and manners.

Omitting those of the pioneer farmers who move from the love of adventure, the advance of the more steady farmer is easy to understand. Obviously the immi-grant was attracted by the cheap lands of the frontier, and even the native farmer felt their influence strongly. Year by year the farmers who lived on soil whose returns were diminished by un-rotated crops were offered the virgin soil of the frontier at nominal prices. Their growing families demanded more lands, and these were dear. The competition of the unexhausted, cheap, and easily tilled prairie lands compelled the farmer either to go west and continue the exhaustion of the soil on a new frontier, or to adopt intensive culture. Thus the census of 1890 shows, in the Northwest, many counties in which there is an absolute or a relative decrease of population. These States have been sending farmers to advance the frontier on the plains, and have them-selves begun to turn to intensive farming and to manufacture. A decade before this, Ohio had shown the same transition stage. Thus the demand for land and the love of wilderness freedom drew the frontier ever onward.

Having now roughly outlined the vari-ous kinds of frontiers, and their modes of advance, chiefly from the point of view of the frontier itself, we may next inquire what were the influences on the East and on the Old World. A rapid enumeration of some of the more note-worthy effects is all that I have time for.

First, we note that the frontier pro-moted the formation of a composite na-tionality for the American people. The coast was preponderantly English, but the later tides of continental immigra-tion flowed across to the free lands. This was the case from the early colonial days. The Scotch-Irish and the Palatine Ger-mans, or "Pennsylvania Dutch," fur-nished the dominant element in the stock of the colonial frontier. With these peoples were also the freed indented servants, or redemptioners, who at the expiration of their time of service passed to the frontier. Governor Spotswood of Virginia writes in 1717, "The inhabitants of our frontiers are composed generally of such as have been transported hither as servants, and, being out of their time, settle themselves where land is to be taken up and that will produce the neces-sarys of life with little labour." Very generally these redemptioners were of non-English stock. In the crucible of the frontier the immigrants were Americanized, liberated, and fused into a mixed race, English in neither nationality nor characteristics. The process has gone on from the early days to our own. Burke and other writers in the middle of the eighteenth century believed that Pennsylvania was "threatened with the danger of being wholly foreign in language, manners and perhaps even inclinations." The German and Scotch-Irish elements in the frontier of the South were only less great. In the middle of the present century the German element in Wisconsin was already so considerable that leading publicists looked to the creation of a German state out of the commonwealth by concentrating their colonization. Such examples teach us to beware of misinterpreting the fact that there is a common English speech in America into a belief that the stock is also English.

In another way the advance of the frontier decreased our dependence on England. The coast, particularly of the South, lacked diversified industries, and was dependent on England for the bulk of its supplies. In the South there was even a dependence on the Northern colonies for articles of food. Governor Glenn, of South Carolina, writes in the middle of the eighteenth century: "Our trade with New York and Philadelphia was of this sort, draining us of all the little money and bills we could gather from other places for their bread, flour, beer, hams, bacon, and other things of their produce, all which, except beer, our new townships begin to supply us with, which are settled with very industrious and thriving Germans. This no doubt diminishes the number of shipping and the appearance of our trade, but it is far from being a detriment to us." Before long the frontier created a demand for merchants. As it retreated from the coast it became less and less possible for England to bring her supplies directly to the consumer's wharfs, and carry away staple crops, and staple crops began to give way to diversified agriculture for a time. The effect of this phase of the frontier action upon the northern section is perceived when we realize how the advance of the frontier aroused seaboard cities like Boston, New York, and Baltimore to engage in rivalry for what Washington called "the extensive and valuable trade of a rising empire."

The legislation which most developed the powers of the national government, and played the largest part in its activity, was conditioned on the frontier. Writers have discussed the subjects of tariff, land, and internal improvement, as subsidiary to the slavery question. But when American history comes to be rightly viewed it will be seen that the slavery question is an incident. In the period from the end of the first half of the present century to the close of the Civil War slavery rose to primary, but far from exclusive, importance. But this does not justify Dr. von Holst (to take an example) in treating our constitutional history in its formative period down to 1828 in a single volume, giving six volumes chiefly to the history of slavery from 1828 to 1861, under the title "Constitutional History of the United States." The growth of nationalism and the evolution of American political institutions were dependent on the advance of the frontier. Even so recent a writer as Rhodes, in his "History of the United States since the Compromise of 1850," has treated the legislation called out by the western advance as incidental to the slavery struggle.

This is a wrong perspective. The pioneer needed the goods of the coast, and so the grand series of internal improvement and railroad legislation began, with potent nationalizing effects. Over internal improvements occurred great debates, in which grave constitutional questions were discussed. Sectional groupings appear in the votes, profoundly significant for the historian. Loose construction increased as the nation marched westward. But the West was not content with bringing the farm to the factory. Under the lead of Clay — "Harry of the West" — protective tariffs were passed, with the cry of bringing the factory to the farm. The disposition of the public lands was a third important subject of national legislation influenced by the frontier.

The public domain has been a force of profound importance in the nationalization and development of the government. The effects of the struggle of the landed and the landless States, and of the Ordinance of 1787, need no discussion. Administratively the frontier called out some of the highest and most vitalizing activities of the general government. The purchase of Louisiana was perhaps the constitutional turning point in the history of the Republic, inasmuch as it afforded both a new area for national legislation and the occasion of the downfall of the policy of strict construction. But the purchase of Louisiana was called out by frontier needs and demands. As frontier States accrued to the Union the national power grew. In a speech on the dedication of the Calhoun monument Mr. Lamar explained: "In 1789 the States were the creators of the Federal Government; in 1861 the Federal Government was the creator of a large majority of the States."

When we consider the public domain from the point of view of the sale and disposal of the public lands we are again brought face to face with the frontier. The policy of the United States in dealing with its lands is in sharp contrast with the European system of scientific administration. Efforts to make this domain a source of revenue, and to withhold it from emigrants in order that settlement might be compact, were in vain. The jealousy and the fears of the East were powerless in the face of the demands of the frontiersmen. John Quincy Adams was obliged to confess: "My own system of administration, which was to make the national domain the inexhaustible fund for progressive and unceasing internal improvement, has failed." The reason is obvious: a system of administration was not what the West demanded; it wanted land. Adams states the situation as follows: "The slaveholders of the South have bought the cooperation of the western country by the bribe of the western lands, abandoning to the new Western States their own proportion of the public property and aiding them in the design of grasping all the lands into their own hands. Thomas H. Benton was the author of this system, which he brought forward as a substitute for the American system of Mr. Clay, and to supplant him as the leading statesman of the West. Mr. Clay, by his tariff compromise with Mr. Calhoun, abandoned his own American system. At the same time he brought forward a plan for distributing among all the States of the Union the proceeds of the sales of the public lands. His bill for that purpose passed both Houses of Congress, but was vetoed by President Jackson, who, in his annual message of December, 1832, formally recommended that all public lands should be gratuitously given away to individual adventurers and to the States in which the lands are situated."

"No subject," said Henry Clay, "which has presented itself to the present, or perhaps any preceding Congress, is of greater magnitude than that of the public lands." When we consider the far-reaching effects of the government's land policy upon political, economic, and social aspects of American life, we are disposed to agree with him. But this legislation was framed under frontier influences, and under the lead of Western statesmen like Benton and Jackson. Said Senator Scott of Indiana in 1841: "I consider the preemption law merely declaratory of the custom or common law of the settlers."

It is safe to say that the legislation with regard to land, tariff, and internal improvements — the American system of the nationalizing Whig party — was conditioned on frontier ideas and needs. But it was not merely in legislative action that the frontier worked against the sectionalism of the coast. The economic and social characteristics of the frontier worked against sectionalism. The men of the frontier had closer resemblances to the Middle region than to either of the other sections. Pennsylvania had been the seed-plot of frontier emigration, and, although she passed on her settlers along the Great Valley into the west of Virginia and the Carolinas, yet the industrial society of these Southern frontiersmen was always more like that of the Middle region than like that of the tide-water portion of the South, which later came to spread its industrial type throughout the South.

The Middle region, entered by New York harbor, was an open door to all Europe. The tide-water part of the South represented typical Englishmen, modified by a warm climate and servile labor, and living in baronial fashion on great plantations; New England stood for a special English movement — Puritanism. The Middle region was less English than the other sections. It had a wide mixture of nationalities, a varied society, the mixed town and county system of local government, a varied economic life, many religious sects. In short, it was a region mediating between New England and the South, and the East and the West. It represented that composite nationality which the contemporary United States exhibits, that juxtaposition of non-English groups, occupying a valley or a little settlement, and presenting reflections of the map of Europe in their variety. It was democratic and non-sectional, if not national; "easy, tolerant, and contented"; rooted strongly in material prosperity. It was typical of the modern United States. It was least sectional, not only because it lay between North and South, but also because with no barriers to shut out its frontiers from its settled region, and with a system of connecting waterways, the Middle region mediated between East and West as well as between North and South. Thus it became the typically American region. Even the New Englander, who was shut out from the frontier by the Middle region, tarrying in New York or Pennsylvania on his westward march, lost the acuteness of his sectionalism on the way.

The spread of cotton culture into the interior of the South finally broke down the contrast between the "tide-water" region and the rest of the State, and based Southern interests on slavery. Before this process revealed its results the western portion of the South, which was akin to Pennsylvania in stock, society, and industry, showed tendencies to fall away from the faith of the fathers into internal improvement legislation and nationalism. In the Virginia convention of 1829–30, called to revise the constitution,

Mr. Leigh, of Chesterfield, one of the tide-water counties, declared:

One of the main causes of discontent which led to this convention, that which had the strongest influence in overcoming our veneration for the work of our fathers, which taught us to contemn the sentiments of Henry and Mason and Pendleton, which weaned us from our reverence for the constituted authorities of the State, was an overweening passion for internal improvement. I say this with perfect knowledge, for it has been avowed to me by gentlemen from the West over and over again. And let me tell the gentleman from Albemarle (Mr. Gordon) that it has been another principal object of those who set this ball of revolution in motion, to overturn the doctrine of State rights, of which Virginia has been the very pillar, and to remove the barrier she has interposed to the interference of the Federal Government in that same work of internal improvement, by so reorganizing the legislature that Virginia, too, may be hitched to the Federal car.

It was this nationalizing tendency of the West that transformed the democracy of Jefferson into the national republicanism of Monroe and the democracy of Andrew Jackson. The West of the War of 1812, the West of Clay, and Benton and Harrison, and Andrew Jackson, shut off by the Middle States and the mountains from the coast sections, had a solidarity of its own with national tendencies. On the tide of the Father of Waters, North and South met and mingled into a nation. Interstate migration went steadily on — a process of cross-fertilization of ideas and institutions. The fierce struggle of the sections over slavery on the western frontier does not diminish the truth of this statement; it proves the truth of it. Slavery was a sectional trait that would not down, but in the West it could not remain sectional. It was the greatest of frontiersmen who

declared: "I believe this Government can not endure permanently half slave and half free. It will become all of one thing or all of the other." Nothing works for nationalism like intercourse within the nation. Mobility of population is death to localism, and the western frontier worked irresistibly in unsettling population. The effect reached back from the frontier and affected profoundly the Atlantic coast and even the Old World.

But the most important effect of the frontier has been in the promotion of democracy here and in Europe. As has been indicated, the frontier is productive of individualism. Complex society is precipitated by the wilderness into a kind of primitive organization based on the family. The tendency is anti-social. It produces antipathy to control, and particularly to any direct control. The tax-gatherer is viewed as a representative of oppression. Prof. Osgood, in an able article, has pointed out that the frontier conditions prevalent in the colonies are important factors in the explanation of the American Revolution, where individual liberty was sometimes confused with absence of all effective government. The same conditions aid in explaining the difficulty of instituting a strong government in the period of the confederacy. The frontier individualism has from the beginning promoted democracy.

The frontier States that came into the Union in the first quarter of a century of its existence came in with democratic suffrage provisions, and had reactive effects of the highest importance upon the older States whose peoples were being attracted there. An extension of the franchise became essential. It was *western* New York that forced an extension of suffrage in the constitutional convention of that State in 1821; and it was *western* Virginia that compelled the tide-water region to put a more liberal suffrage provision in the constitution framed in 1830, and to give to the frontier region a more nearly proportionate representation with the tide-water aristocracy. The rise of democracy as an effective force in the nation came in with western preponderance under Jackson and William Henry Harrison, and it meant the triumph of the frontier — with all of its good and with all of its evil elements. An interesting illustration of the tone of frontier democracy in 1830 comes from the same debates in the Virginia convention already referred to. A representative from western Virginia declared:

But, sir, it is not the increase of population in the West which this gentleman ought to fear. It is the energy which the mountain breeze and western habits impart to those emigrants. They are regenerated, politically I mean, sir. They soon become *working politicians;* and the difference, sir, between a *talking* and a *working* politician is immense. The Old Dominion has long been celebrated for producing great orators; the ablest metaphysicians in policy; men that can split hairs in all abstruse questions of political economy. But at home, or when they return from Congress, they have negroes to fan them asleep. But a Pennsylvania, a New York, an Ohio, or a western Virginia statesman, though far inferior in logic, metaphysics, and rhetoric to an old Virginia statesman, has this advantage, that when he returns home he takes off his coat and takes hold of the plow. This gives him bone and muscle, sir, and preserves his republican principles pure and uncontaminated.

So long as free land exists, the opportunity for a competency exists, and economic power secures political power. But the democracy born of free land, strong in selfishness and individualism, intolerant of administrative experience and education, and pressing individual liberty beyond its proper bounds, has its dangers as well as its benefits. Individualism in America has allowed a laxity in regard to governmental affairs which has rendered possible the spoils system and all the manifest evils that follow from the lack of a highly developed civic spirit. In this connection may be noted also the influence of frontier conditions in permitting lax business honor, inflated paper currency and wild-cat banking. The colonial and revolutionary frontier was the region whence emanated many of the worst forms of an evil currency. The West in the War of 1812 repeated the phenomenon on the frontier of that day, while the speculation and wild-cat banking of the period of the crisis of 1837 occurred on the new frontier belt of the next tier of States. Thus each one of the periods of lax financial integrity coincides with periods when a new set of frontier communities had arisen, and coincides in area with these successive frontiers, for the most part. The recent Populist agitation is a case in point. Many a State that now declines any connection with the tenets of the Populists, itself adhered to such ideas in an earlier stage of the development of the State. A primitive society can hardly be expected to show the intelligent appreciation of the complexity of business interests in a developed society. The continual recurrence of these areas of paper-money agitation is another evidence that the frontier can be isolated and studied as a factor in American history of the highest importance.

The East has always feared the result of an unregulated advance of the frontier, and has tried to check and guide it. The English authorities would have checked settlement at the headwaters of the Atlantic tributaries and allowed the "savages to enjoy their deserts in quiet lest the peltry trade should decrease." This called out Burke's splendid protest:

If you stopped your grants, what would be the consequence? The people would occupy without grants. They have already so occupied in many places. You can not station garrisons in every part of these deserts. If you drive the people from one place, they will carry on their annual tillage and remove with their flocks and herds to another. Many of the people in the back settlements are already little attached to particular situations. Already they have topped the Appalachian Mountains. From thence they behold before them an immense plain, one vast, rich level meadow; a square of five hundred miles. Over this they would wander without a possibility of restraint; they would change their manners with their habits of life; would soon forget a government by which they were disowned; would become hordes of English Tartars; and, pouring down upon your unfortified frontiers a fierce and irresistible cavalry, become masters of your governors and your counselers, your collectors and comptrollers, and of all the slaves that adhered to them. Such would, and in no long time must, be the effect of attempting to forbid as a crime and to suppress as an evil the command and blessing of Providence, "Increase and multiply." Such would be the happy result of an endeavor to keep as a lair of wild beasts that earth which God, by an express charter, has given to the children of men.

But the English Government was not alone in its desire to limit the advance of the frontier and guide its destinies. Tide-water Virginia and South Carolina gerrymandered those colonies to insure the dominance of the coast in their legislatures. Washington desired to settle a State at a time in the Northwest; Jefferson would reserve from settlement the territory of his Louisiana Purchase north of the thirty-second parallel, in order to offer it to the Indians in exchange for their settlements east of the Mississippi.

"When we shall be full on this side," he writes, "we may lay off a range of States on the western bank from the head to the mouth, and so range after range, advancing compactly as we multiply." Madison went so far as to argue to the French minister that the United States had no interest in seeing population extend itself on the right bank of the Mississippi, but should rather fear it. When the Oregon question was under debate, in 1824, Smyth, of Virginia, would draw an unchangeable line for the limits of the United States at the outer limit of two tiers of States beyond the Mississippi, complaining that the seaboard States were being drained of the flower of their population by the bringing of too much land into market. Even Thomas Benton, the man of widest views of the destiny of the West, at this stage of his career declared that along the ridge of the Rocky Mountains "the western limits of the Republic should be drawn, and the statue of the fabled god Terminus should be raised upon its highest peak, never to be thrown down." But the attempts to limit the boundaries, to restrict land sales and settlement, and to deprive the West of its share of political power were all in vain. Steadily the frontier of settlement advanced and carried with it individualism, democracy, and nationalism, and powerfully affected the East and the Old World.

The most effective efforts of the East to regulate the frontier came through its educational and religious activity, exerted by interstate migration and by organized societies. Speaking in 1835, Dr. Lyman Beecher declared: "It is equally plain that the religious and political destiny of our nation is to be decided in the West," and he pointed out that the population of the West "is assembled from all the States of the

Union and from all the nations of Europe, and is rushing in like the waters of the flood, demanding for its moral preservation the immediate and universal action of those institutions which discipline the mind and arm the conscience and the heart. And so various are the opinions and habits, and so recent and imperfect is the acquaintance, and so sparse are the settlements of the West, that no homogeneous public sentiment can be formed to legislate immediately into being the requisite institutions. And yet they are all needed immediately in their utmost perfection and power. A nation is being 'born in a day.'... But what will become of the West if her prosperity rushes up to such a majesty of power, while those great institutions linger which are necessary to form the mind and the conscience and the heart of that vast world? It must not be permitted.... Let no man at the East quiet himself and dream of liberty, whatever may become of the West.... Her destiny is our destiny."

With the appeal to the conscience of New England, he adds appeals to her fears lest other religious sects anticipate her own. The New England preacher and school-teacher left their mark on the West. The dread of Western emancipation from New England's political and economic control was paralleled by her fears lest the West cut loose from her religion. Commenting in 1850 on reports that settlement was rapidly extending northward in Wisconsin, the editor of the *Home Missionary* writes: "We scarcely know whether to rejoice or mourn over this extension of our settlements. While we sympathize in whatever tends to increase the physical resources and prosperity of our country, we can not forget that with all these dispersions into remote and still remoter corners of the land

the supply of the means of grace is becoming relatively less and less." Acting in accordance with such ideas, home missions were established and Western colleges were erected. As seaboard cities like Philadelphia, New York, and Baltimore strove for the mastery of Western trade, so the various denominations strove for the possession of the West. Thus an intellectual stream from New England sources fertilized the West. Other sections sent their missionaries; but the real struggle was between sects. The contest for power and the expansive tendency furnished to the various sects by the existence of a moving frontier must have had important results on the character of religious organization in the United States. The multiplication of rival churches in the little frontier towns had deep and lasting social effects. The religious aspects of the frontier make a chapter in our history which needs study.

From the conditions of frontier life came intellectual traits of profound importance. The works of travelers along each frontier from colonial days onward describe certain common traits, and these traits have, while softening down, still persisted as survivals in the place of their origin, even when a higher social organization succeeded. The result is that to the frontier the American intellect owes its striking characteristics. That coarseness and strength combined with acuteness and inquisitiveness; that practical, inventive turn of mind, quick to find expedients; that masterful grasp of material things, lacking in the artistic but powerful to effect great ends; that restless, nervous energy; that dominant individualism, working for good and for evil, and withal that buoyancy and exuberance which comes with freedom — these are traits of the frontier, or traits called out elsewhere because of the existence of the frontier. Since the days when the fleet of Columbus sailed into the waters of the New World, America has been another name for opportunity, and the people of the United States have taken their tone from the incessant expansion which has not only been open but has even been forced upon them. He would be a rash prophet who should assert that the expansive character of American life has now entirely ceased. Movement has been its dominant fact, and, unless this training has no effect upon a people, the American energy will continually demand a wider field for its exercise. But never again will such gifts of free land offer themselves. For a moment, at the frontier, the bonds of custom are broken and unrestraint is triumphant. There is not *tabula rasa*. The stubborn American environment is there with its imperious summons to accept its conditions; the inherited ways of doing things are also there; and yet, in spite of environment, and in spite of custom, each frontier did indeed furnish a new field of opportunity, a gate of escape from the bondage of the past; and freshness, and confidence, and scorn of older society, impatience of its restraints and its ideas, and indifference to its lessons, have accompanied the frontier. What the Mediterranean Sea was to the Greeks, breaking the bond of custom, offering new experiences, calling out new institutions and activities, that, and more, the ever retreating frontier has been to the United States directly, and to the nations of Europe more remotely. And now, four centuries from the discovery of America, at the end of a hundred years of life under the Constitution, the frontier has gone, and with its going has closed the first period of American history.

Frederick Jackson Turner:

CONTRIBUTIONS OF THE WEST
TO AMERICAN DEMOCRACY

POLITICAL thought in the period of the French Revolution tended to treat democracy as an absolute system applicable to all times and to all peoples, a system that was to be created by the act of the people themselves on philosophical principles. Ever since that era there has been an inclination on the part of writers on democracy to emphasize the analytical and theoretical treatment to the neglect of the underlying factors of historical development.

If, however, we consider the underlying conditions and forces that create the democratic type of government, and at times contradict the external forms to which the name democracy is applied, we shall find that under this name there have appeared a multitude of political types radically unlike in fact.

The careful student of history must, therefore, seek the explanation of the forms and changes of political institutions in the social and economic forces that determine them. To know that at any one time a nation may be called a democracy, an aristocracy, or a monarchy, is not so important as to know what are the social and economic tendencies of the state. These are the vital forces that work beneath the surface and dominate the external form. It is to changes in the economic and social life of a people that we must look for the forces that ultimately create and modify organs of political action. For the time, adaptation of political structure may be incomplete or concealed. Old organs will be utilized to express new forces, and so gradual and subtle will be the change that it may hardly be recognized. The pseudo-democracies under the Medici at Florence and under Augustus at Rome are familiar examples of this type. Or again, if the political structure be rigid, incapable of responding to the changes demanded by growth, the expansive forces of social and economic transformation may rend it in some catastrophe like that of the French Revolution. In all these changes both conscious ideals and unconscious social reorganization are at work.

These facts are familiar to the student, and yet it is doubtful if they have been fully considered in connection with American democracy. For a century at least, in conventional expression, Americans have referred to a "glorious Constitution" in explaining the stability and prosperity of their democracy. We have believed as a nation that other peoples had only to will our democratic institutions in order to repeat our own career.

From *The Frontier in American History* by Frederick Jackson Turner, copyright 1920 by Frederick Jackson Turner, copyright 1948 by Caroline M. S. Turner. Reprinted by permission of Henry Holt and Company, Inc.

In dealing with Western contributions to democracy, it is essential that the considerations which have just been mentioned shall be kept in mind. Whatever these contributions may have been, we find ourselves at the present time in an era of such profound economic and social transformation as to raise the question of the effect of these changes upon the democratic institutions of the United States. Within a decade four marked changes have occurred in our national development; taken together they constitute a revolution.

First, there is the exhaustion of the supply of free land and the closing of the movement of Western advance as an effective factor in American development. The first rough conquest of the wilderness is accomplished, and that great supply of free lands which year after year has served to reinforce the democratic influences in the United States is exhausted. It is true that vast tracts of government land are still untaken, but they constitute the mountain and arid regions, only a small fraction of them capable of conquest, and then only by the application of capital and combined effort. The free lands that made the American pioneer have gone.

In the second place, contemporaneously with this there has been such a concentration of capital in the control of fundamental industries as to make a new epoch in the economic development of the United States. The iron, the coal, and the cattle of the country have all fallen under the domination of a few great corporations with allied interests, and by the rapid combination of the important railroad systems and steamship lines, in concert with these same forces, even the breadstuffs and the manufactures of the nation are to some degree controlled in a similar way. This is largely the work of the last decade. The development of the greatest iron mines of Lake Superior occurred in the early nineties, and in the same decade came the combination by which the coal and the coke of the country, and the transportation systems that connect them with the iron mines, have been brought under a few concentrated managements. Side by side with this concentration of capital has gone the combination of labor in the same vast industries. The one is in a certain sense the concomitant of the other, but the movement acquires an additional significance because of the fact that during the past fifteen years the labor class has been so recruited by a tide of foreign immigration that this class is now largely made up of persons of foreign parentage, and the lines of cleavage which begin to appear in this country between capital and labor have been accentuated by distinctions of nationality.

A third phenomenon connected with the two just mentioned is the expansion of the United States politically and commercially into lands beyond the seas. A cycle of American development has been completed. Up to the close of the War of 1812, this country was involved in the fortunes of the European state system. The first quarter of a century of our national existence was almost a continual struggle to prevent ourselves being drawn into the European wars. At the close of that era of conflict, the United States set its face toward the West. It began the settlement and improvement of the vast interior of the country. Here was the field of our colonization, here the field of our political activity. This process being completed, it is not strange that we find the United States again involved in world-politics. The revolution that occurred four years ago, when the United States struck down that ancient nation under whose auspices the New World was discovered, is hardly yet more than dimly understood. The insular wreckage of the Spanish War, Porto Rico and the Philippines, with the problems presented by the Hawaiian Islands, Cuba, the Isthmian Canal, and China, all are indications of the new direction of the ship of state, and while we thus turn our attention overseas, our concentrated industrial strength has given us a striking power against the commerce of Europe that is already producing consternation in the Old World. Having completed the conquest of the wilderness, and having consolidated our interests, we are beginning to consider the relations of democracy and empire.

And fourth, the political parties of the United States now tend to divide on issues that involve the question of Socialism. The rise of the Populist party in the last decade, and the acceptance of so many of its principles by the Democratic party under the leadership of Mr. Bryan, show in striking manner the birth of new political ideas, the reformation of the lines of political conflict.

It is doubtful if in any ten years of American history more significant factors in our growth have revealed themselves. The struggle of the pioneer farmers to subdue the arid lands of the Great Plains in the eighties was followed by the official announcement of the extinction of the frontier line in 1890. The dramatic outcome of the Chicago Convention of 1896 marked the rise into power of the representatives of Populistic change. Two years later came the battle of Manila, which broke down the old isolation of the nation, and started it on a path the goal of which no man can foretell; and finally, but two years ago came that concentration of which the billion and a half dollar steel trust and the union of the

Northern continental railways are stupendous examples. Is it not obvious, then, that the student who seeks for the explanation of democracy in the social and economic forces that underlie political forms must make inquiry into the conditions that have produced our democratic institutions, if he would estimate the effect of these vast changes? As a contribution to this inquiry, let us now turn to an examination of the part that the West has played in shaping our democracy.

From the beginning of the settlement of America, the frontier regions have exercised a steady influence toward democracy. In Virginia, to take an example, it can be traced as early as the period of Bacon's Rebellion, a hundred years before our Declaration of Independence. The small landholders, seeing that their powers were steadily passing into the hands of the wealthy planters who controlled Church and State and lands, rose in revolt. A generation later, in the governorship of Alexander Spotswood, we find a contest between the frontier settlers and the property-holding classes of the coast. The democracy with which Spotswood had to struggle, and of which he so bitterly complained, was a democracy made up of small landholders, of the newer immigrants, and of indented servants, who at the expiration of their time of servitude passed into the interior to take up lands and engage in pioneer farming. The "War of the Regulation," just on the eve of the American Revolution, shows the steady persistence of this struggle between the classes of the interior and those of the coast. The Declaration of Grievances which the back counties of the Carolinas then drew up against the aristocracy that dominated the politics of those colonies exhibits the contest between the democracy of the frontier and the established classes who apportioned the legislature in such fashion as to secure effective control of government. Indeed, in the period before the outbreak of the American Revolution, one can trace a distinct belt of democratic territory extending from the back country of New England down through western New York, Pennsylvania, and the South.

In each colony this region was in conflict with the dominant classes of the coast. It constituted a quasi-revolutionary area before the days of the Revolution, and it formed the basis on which the Democratic party was afterwards established. It was, therefore, in the West, as it was in the period before the Declaration of Independence, that the struggle for democratic development first revealed itself, and in that area the essential ideas of American democracy had already appeared. Through the period of the Revolution and of the Confederation a similar contest can be noted. On the frontier of New England, along the western border of Pennsylvania, Virginia, and the Carolinas, and in the communities beyond the Allegheny Mountains, there arose a demand of the frontier settlers for independent statehood based on democratic provisions. There is a strain of fierceness in their energetic petitions demanding self-government under the theory that every people have the right to establish their own political institutions in an area which they have won from the wilderness. Those revolutionary principles based on natural rights, for which the seaboard colonies were contending, were taken up with frontier energy in an attempt to apply them to the lands of the West. No one can read their petitions denouncing the control exercised by the wealthy landholders of the coast, appealing to the record of their conquest of the wilderness, and demanding the possession of the lands for which they have fought the Indians, and which they had reduced by their ax to civilization, without recognizing in these frontier communities the cradle of a belligerent Western democracy. "A fool can sometimes put on his coat better than a wise man can do it for him," — such is the philosophy of its petitioners. In this period also came the contests of the interior agricultural portion of New England against the coastwise merchants and property-holders, of which Shays' Rebellion is the best known, although by no means an isolated instance.

By the time of the constitutional convention, this struggle for democracy had effected a fairly well-defined division into parties. Although these parties did not at first recognize their interstate connections, there were similar issues on which they split in almost all the States. The demands for an issue of paper money, the stay of execution against debtors, and the relief against excessive taxation were found in every colony in the interior agricultural regions. The rise of this significant movement wakened the apprehensions of the men of means, and in the debates over the basis of suffrage for the House of Representatives in the constitutional convention of 1787 leaders of the conservative party did not hesitate to demand that safeguards to the property should be furnished the coast against the interior. The outcome of the debate left the question of suffrage for the House of Representatives dependent upon the policy of the separate States. This was in effect imposing a property qualification throughout the nation as a whole, and it was only as the interior of the country developed that these restrictions gradually gave way in the direction of manhood suffrage.

All of these scattered democratic tendencies Jefferson combined, in the period of Washington's presidency, into the Democratic-Republican party. Jefferson was the first prophet of American democracy, and when we analyse the essential features of his gospel, it is clear that the Western influence was the dominant element. Jefferson himself was born in the frontier region of Virginia, on the edge of the Blue Ridge, in the middle of the eighteenth century. His father was a pioneer. Jefferson's "Notes on Virginia" reveal clearly his conception that democracy should have an agricultural basis, and that manufacturing development and city life were dangerous to the purity of the body politic. Simplicity and economy in government, the right of revolution, the freedom of the individual, the belief that those who win the vacant lands are entitled to shape their own government in their own way, — these are all parts of the platform of political principles to which he gave his adhesion, and they are all elements eminently characteristic of the Western democracy into which he was born.

In the period of the Revolution he had brought in a series of measures which tended to throw the power of Virginia into the hands of the settlers in the interior rather than of the coastwise aristocracy. The repeal of the laws of entail and primogeniture would have destroyed the great estates on which the planting aristocracy based its power. The abolition of the Established Church would still further have diminished the influence of the coastwise party in favor of the dissenting sects of the interior. His scheme of general public education reflected the same tendency, and his demand for the abolition of slavery was characteristic of a representative of the West rather than of the old-time aristocracy of the coast. His sympathy with the Western expansion culminated in the Louisiana Purchase. In short, the tendencies of Jefferson's legislation were to replace the dominance of the planting aristocracy by the dominance of the interior class, which had sought in vain to achieve its liberties in the period of Bacon's Rebellion.

Nevertheless, Thomas Jefferson was the John the Baptist of democracy, not its Moses. Only with the slow setting of the tide of settlement farther and farther toward the interior did the democratic influence grow strong enough to take actual possession of the government. The period from 1800 to 1820 saw a steady increase in these tendencies. The established classes in New England and the South began to take alarm. Perhaps no better illustration of the apprehensions of the old-time Federal conservative can be given than these utterances of President Dwight, of Yale College, in the book of travels which he published in that period:

The class of pioneers cannot live in regular society. They are too idle, too talkative, too passionate, too prodigal, and too shiftless to acquire either property or character. They are impatient of the restraints of law, religion, and morality, and grumble about the taxes by which the Rulers, Ministers, and Schoolmasters are supported. . . . After exposing the injustice of the community in neglecting to invest persons of such superior merit in public offices, in many an eloquent harangue uttered by many a kitchen fire, in every blacksmith shop, in every corner of the streets, and finding all their efforts vain, they become at length discouraged, and under the pressure of poverty, the fear of the gaol, and consciousness of public contempt, leave their native places and betake themselves to the wilderness.

Such was a conservative's impression of that pioneer movement of New England colonists who had spread up the valley of the Connecticut into New Hampshire, Vermont, and western New York in the period of which he wrote, and who afterwards went on to possess the Northwest. New England Federalism looked with a shudder at the democratic ideas of those who refused to recognize the established order. But in that period there came into the Union a sisterhood of frontier States — Ohio, Indiana, Illinois, Missouri — with provisions for the franchise that brought in complete democracy.

Even the newly created States of the Southwest showed the tendency. The wind of democracy blew so strongly from the West, that even in the older States of New York, Massachusetts, Connecticut, and Virginia, conventions were called, which liberalized their constitutions by strengthening the democratic basis of the State. In the same time the labor population of the cities began to assert its power and its determination to share in government. Of this frontier democracy which now took possession of the nation, Andrew Jackson was the very personification. He was born in the backwoods of the Carolinas in the midst of the turbulent democracy that preceded the Revolution, and he grew up in the frontier State of Tennessee. In the midst of this region of personal feuds and frontier ideals of law, he quickly rose to leadership. The appearance of this frontiersman on the floor of Congress was an omen full of significance. He reached Philadelphia at the close of Washington's administration, having ridden on horseback nearly eight hundred miles to his destination. Gallatin, himself a Western man, describes Jackson as he entered the halls of Congress: "A tall, lank, uncouth-looking personage, with long locks of hair hanging over his face and a cue down his back tied in an eel-skin; his dress singular; his manners those of a rough backwoodsman." And Jefferson testified: "When I was President of the Senate he was a Senator, and he could never speak on account of the rashness of his feelings. I have seen him attempt it repeatedly and as often choke with rage." At last the frontier in the person of its typical man had found a place in the Government. This six-foot backwoodsman, with blue eyes that could blaze on occasion, this choleric, impetuous, self-willed Scotch-Irish leader of men, this expert duelist, and ready fighter, this embodiment of the tenacious, vehement, personal West, was in politics to stay. The frontier democracy of that time had the instincts of the clansman in the days of Scotch border warfare. Vehement and tenacious as the democracy was, strenuously as each man contended with his neighbor for the spoils of the new country that opened before them, they all had respect for the man who best expressed their aspirations and their ideas. Every community had its hero. In the War of 1812 and the subsequent Indian fighting Jackson made good his claim, not only to the loyalty of the people of Tennessee, but of the whole West, and even of the nation. He had the essential traits of the Kentucky and Tennessee frontier. It was a frontier free from the influence of European ideas and institutions. The men of the "Western World" turned their backs upon the Atlantic Ocean, and with a grim energy and self-reliance began to build up a society free from the dominance of ancient forms.

The Westerner defended himself and resented governmental restrictions. The duel and the blood-feud found congenial soil in Kentucky and Tennessee. The idea of the personality of law was often dominant over the organized machinery of justice. That method was best which was most direct and effective. The backwoodsman was intolerant of men who split hairs, or scrupled over the method of reaching the right. In a word, the unchecked development of the individual was the significant product of this frontier democracy. It sought rather to express itself by choosing a man of the people, than by the formation of elaborate governmental institutions.

It was because Andrew Jackson personified these essential Western traits that in his presidency he became the idol and the mouthpiece of the popular will. In his assault upon the Bank as an engine of aristocracy, and in his denunciation of nullification, he went directly to his object with the ruthless energy of a frontiersman. For formal law and the subtleties of State sovereignty he had the contempt of a backwoodsman. Nor is it without significance that this typical man of the new democracy will always be associated with the triumph of the spoils system in national politics. To the new democracy of the West, office was an opportunity to exercise natural rights as an equal citizen of the community. Rotation in office served not simply to allow the successful man to punish his enemies and reward his friends but it also furnished the training in the actual conduct of political affairs which every American claimed as his birthright. Only in a primitive democracy of the type of the United States in 1830 could such a system have existed without the ruin of the State. National government in that period was no complex and nicely adjusted machine, and the evils of the system were long in making themselves fully apparent.

The triumph of Andrew Jackson marked the end of the old era of trained statesmen for the Presidency. With him began the era of the popular hero. Even Martin Van Buren, whom we think of in connection with the East, was born in a log house under conditions that were not unlike parts of the older West. Harrison was the hero of the Northwest, as Jackson had been of the Southwest. Polk was a typical Tennesseean, eager to expand the nation, and Zachary Taylor was what Webster called a "frontier colonel." During the period that followed Jackson, power passed from the region of Kentucky and Tennessee to the border of the Mississippi. The natural democratic tendencies that had earlier shown themselves in the Gulf States were destroyed, however, by the spread of cotton culture, and the development of great plantations in that region. What had been typical of the democracy of the Revolutionary frontier and of the frontier of Andrew Jackson was now to be seen in the States between the Ohio and the Mississippi. As Andrew Jackson is the typical democrat of the former region, so Abraham Lincoln is the very embodiment of the pioneer period of the Old Northwest. Indeed, he is the embodiment of the democracy of the West. How can one speak of him except in the words of Lowell's great "Commemoration Ode": —

"For him her Old-World moulds aside she
       threw,
And, choosing sweet clay from the breast
     Of the unexhausted West,

With stuff untainted shaped a hero new,
Wise, steadfast in the strength of God, and
   true.

. . . .

His was no lonely mountain-peak of mind,
Thrusting to thin air o'er our cloudy bars,
A sea-mark now, now lost in vapors blind;
Broad prairie rather, genial, level-lined,
Fruitful and friendly for all human kind,
Yet also nigh to heaven and loved of loftiest
   stars.
   Nothing of Europe here,
Or, then, of Europe fronting mornward still,
Ere any names of Serf and Peer
Could Nature's equal scheme deface;
New birth of our new soil, the first American."

The pioneer life from which Lincoln
came differed in important respects from
the frontier democracy typified by Andrew Jackson. Jackson's democracy was
contentious, individualistic, and it sought
the ideal of local self-government and
expansion. Lincoln represents rather the
pioneer folk who entered the forest of
the great Northwest to chop out a home,
to build up their fortunes in the midst
of a continually ascending industrial
movement. In the democracy of the
Southwest, industrial development and
city life were only minor factors, but to
the democracy of the Northwest they
were its very life. To widen the area of
the clearing, to contend with one another
for the mastery of the industrial resources of the rich provinces, to struggle
for a place in the ascending movement
of society, to transmit to one's offspring
the chance for education, for industrial
betterment, for the rise in life which the
hardships of the pioneer existence denied
to the pioneer himself, these were some
of the ideals of the region to which Lincoln came. The men were commonwealth
builders, industry builders. Whereas the
type of hero in the Southwest was mili-
tant, in the Northwest he was industrial. It

was in the midst of these "plain people,"
as he loved to call them, that Lincoln
grew to manhood. As Emerson says:
"He is the true history of the American
people in his time." The years of his
early life were the years when the democracy of the Northwest came into
struggle with the institution of slavery
which threatened to forbid the expansion
of the democratic pioneer life in the
West. In President Eliot's essay on "Five
American Contributions to Civilization,"
he instances as one of the supreme tests
of American democracy its attitude upon
the question of slavery. But if democracy chose wisely and worked effectively
toward the solution of this problem, it
must be remembered that Western democracy took the lead. The rail-splitter
himself became the nation's President in
that fierce time of struggle, and armies
of the woodsmen and pioneer farmers
recruited in the Old Northwest made
free the Father of Waters, marched
through Georgia, and helped to force the
struggle to a conclusion at Appomattox.
The free pioneer democracy struck down
the slave-holding aristocracy on its march
to the West.

The last chapter in the development
of Western democracy is the one that
deals with its conquest over the vast
spaces of the new West. At each new
stage of Western development, the
people have had to grapple with larger
areas, with bigger combinations. The
little colony of Massachusetts veterans
that settled at Marietta received a land
grant as large as the State of Rhode
Island. The band of Connecticut pioneers that followed Moses Cleaveland to
the Connecticut Reserve occupied a region as large as the parent State. The
area which settlers of New England stock
occupied on the prairies of northern Illinois surpassed the combined area of

Massachusetts, Connecticut, and Rhode Island. Men who had become accustomed to the narrow valleys and the little towns of the East found themselves out on the boundless spaces of the West dealing with units of such magnitude as dwarfed their former experience. The Great Lakes, the Prairies, the Great Plains, the Rocky Mountains, the Mississippi and the Missouri, furnished new standards of measurement for the achievement of this industrial democracy. Individualism began to give way to cooperation and to governmental activity. Even in the earlier days of the democratic conquest of the wilderness, demands had been made upon the government for support in internal improvements, but this new West showed a growing tendency to call to its assistance the powerful arm of national authority. In the period since the Civil War, the vast public domain has been donated to the individual farmer, to States for education, to railroads for the construction of transportation lines.

Moreover, with the advent of democracy in the last fifteen years upon the Great Plains, new physical conditions have presented themselves which have accelerated the social tendency of Western democracy. The pioneer farmer of the days of Lincoln could place his family on a flatboat, strike into the wilderness, cut out his clearing, and with little or no capital go on to the achievement of industrial independence. Even the homesteader on the Western prairies found it possible to work out a similar independent destiny, although the factor of transportation made a serious and increasing impediment to the free working-out of his individual career. But when the arid lands and the mineral resources of the Far West were reached, no conquest was possible by the old individual

pioneer methods. Here expensive irrigation works must be constructed, cooperative activity was demanded in utilization of the water supply, capital beyond the reach of the small farmer was required. In a word, the physiographic province itself decreed that the destiny of this new frontier should be social rather than individual.

Magnitude of social achievement is the watchword of the democracy since the Civil War. From petty towns built in the marshes, cities arose whose greatness and industrial power are the wonder of our time. The conditions were ideal for the production of captains of industry. The old democratic admiration for the self-made man, its old deference to the rights of competitive individual development, together with the stupendous natural resources that opened to the conquest of the keenest and the strongest, gave such conditions of mobility as enabled the development of the large corporate industries which in our own decade have marked the West.

Thus, in brief, have been outlined the chief phases of the development of Western democracy in the different areas which it has conquered. There has been a steady development of the industrial ideal, and a steady increase of the social tendency, in this later movement of Western democracy. While the individualism of the frontier, so prominent in the earliest days of the Western advance, has been preserved as an ideal, more and more these individuals struggling each with the other, dealing with vaster and vaster areas, with larger and larger problems, have found it necessary to combine under the leadership of the strongest. This is the explanation of the rise of those preeminent captains of industry whose genius has concentrated capital to control the fundamental resources of the nation. If now in the way of recapitulation we try to pick out from the influences that have gone to the making of Western democracy the factors which constitute the net result of this movement, we shall have to mention at least the following: —

Most important of all has been the fact that an area of free land has continually lain on the western border of the settled area of the United States. Whenever social conditions tended to crystallize in the East, whenever capital tended to press upon labor or political restraints to impede the freedom of the mass, there was this gate of escape to the free conditions of the frontier. These free lands promoted individualism, economic equality, freedom to rise, democracy. Men would not accept inferior wages and a permanent position of social subordination when this promised land of freedom and equality was theirs for the taking. Who would rest content under oppressive legislative conditions when with a slight effort he might reach a land wherein to become a co-worker in the building of free cities and free States on the lines of his own ideal? In a word, then, free lands meant free opportunities. Their existence has differentiated the American democracy from the democracies which have preceded it, because ever, as democracy in the East took the form of highly specialized and complicated industrial society, in the West it kept in touch with primitive conditions, and by action and reaction these two forces have shaped our history.

In the next place, these free lands and this treasury of industrial resources have existed over such vast spaces that they have demanded of democracy increasing spaciousness of design and power of execution. Western democracy is contrasted with the democracy of all other times in the largeness of the tasks to which it has set its hand, and in the vast achievements which it has wrought out in the control of nature and of politics. It would be difficult to over-emphasize the importance of this training upon democracy. Never before in the history of the world has a democracy existed on so vast an area and handled things in the gross with such success, with such largeness of design, and such grasp upon the means of execution. In short, democracy has learned in the West of the United States how to deal with the problem of magnitude. The old historic democracies were but little states with primitive economic conditions.

But the very task of dealing with vast resources, over vast areas, under the conditions of free competition furnished by the West, has produced the rise of those captains of industry whose success in consolidating economic power now raises the question as to whether democracy under such conditions can survive. For the old military type of Western leaders like George Rogers Clark, Andrew Jackson, and William Henry Harrison have been substituted such industrial leaders as James J. Hill, John D. Rockefeller, and Andrew Carnegie.

The question is imperative, then, What ideals persist from this democratic experience of the West; and have they acquired sufficient momentum to sustain themselves under conditions so radically unlike those in the days of their origin? In other words, the question put at the beginning of this discussion becomes pertinent. Under the forms of the American democracy is there in reality evolving such a concentration of economic and social power in the hands of a comparatively few men as may make political democracy an appearance rather than a reality? The free lands are gone. The material forces that gave vitality to Western democracy are passing away. It is to the realm of the spirit, to the domain of ideals and legislation, that we must look for Western influence upon democracy in our own days.

Western democracy has been from the time of its birth idealistic. The very fact of the wilderness appealed to men as a fair, blank page on which to write a new chapter in the story of man's struggle for a higher type of society. The Western wilds, from the Alleghenies to the Pacific, constituted the richest free gift that was ever spread out before civilized man. To the peasant and artisan of the Old World, bound by the chains of social class, as old as custom and as inevitable as fate, the West offered an exit into a free life and greater well-being among the bounties of nature, into the midst of resources that demanded manly exertion, and that gave in return the chance for indefinite ascent in the scale of social advance. "To each she offered gifts after his will." Never again can such an opportunity come to the sons of men. It was unique, and the thing is so near us, so much a part of our lives, that we do not even yet comprehend its full significance. The existence of this land of opportunity has made America the goal of idealists from the days of the Pilgrim Fathers. With all the materialism of the pioneer movements, this idealistic conception of the vacant lands as an opportunity for a new order of things is unmistakably present. Kipling's "Song of the English" has given it expression: —

"We were dreamers, dreaming greatly, in the
    man-stifled town;
We yearned beyond the sky-line where the
    strange roads go down.
Came the Whisper, came the Vision, came
    the Power with the Need,

Till the Soul that is not man's soul was lent
    us to lead.
As the deer breaks — as the steer breaks —
    from the herd where they graze,
In the faith of little children we went on our
    ways.
Then the wood failed — then the food failed
    — then the last water dried —
In the faith of little children we lay down and
    died.

"On the sand-drift — on the veldt-side — in
    the fern-scrub we lay,
That our sons might follow after by the bones
    on the way.
Follow after — follow after! We have watered
    the root
And the bud has come to blossom that ripens
    for fruit!
Follow after — we are waiting by the trails
    that we lost
For the sound of many footsteps, for the
    tread of a host.

"Follow after — follow after — for the harvest is sown:
By the bones about the wayside ye shall come
    to your own!"

This was the vision that called to Roger Williams, — that "prophetic soul ravished of truth disembodied," "unable to enter into treaty with its environment," and forced to seek the wilderness. "Oh, how sweet," wrote William Penn, from his forest refuge, "is the quiet of these parts, freed from the troubles and perplexities of woeful Europe." And here he projected what he called his "Holy Experiment in Government."

If the later West offers few such striking illustrations of the relation of the wilderness to idealistic schemes, and if some of the designs were fantastic and abortive, none the less the influence is a fact. Hardly a Western State but has been the Mecca of some sect or band of social reformers, anxious to put into practice their ideals, in vacant land, far removed from the checks of a settled form of social organization. Consider the Dunkards, the Icarians, the Fourierists, the Mormons, and similar idealists who sought our Western wilds. But the idealistic influence is not limited to the dreamers' conception of a new State. It gave to the pioneer farmer and city builder a restless energy, a quick capacity for judgment and action, a belief in liberty, freedom of opportunity, and a resistance to the domination of class which infused a vitality and power into the individual atoms of this democratic mass. Even as he dwelt among the stumps of his newly-cut clearing, the pioneer had the creative vision of a new order of society. In imagination he pushed back the forest boundary to the confines of a mighty Commonwealth; he willed that log cabins should become the lofty buildings of great cities. He decreed that his children should enter into a heritage of education, comfort, and social welfare, and for this ideal he bore the scars of the wilderness. Possessed with this idea he ennobled his task and laid deep foundations for a democratic State. Nor was this idealism by any means limited to the American pioneer.

To the old native democratic stock has been added a vast army of recruits from the Old World. There are in the Middle West alone four million persons of German parentage out of a total of seven millions in the country. Over a million persons of Scandinavian parentage live in the same region. The democracy of the newer West is deeply affected by the ideals brought by these immigrants from the Old World. To them America was not simply a new home; it was a land of opportunity, of freedom, of democracy. It meant to them, as to the American pioneer that preceded them, the opportunity to destroy the bonds of social caste that bound them in their older home, to hew out for themselves in a new country a destiny proportioned to the powers that God had given them, a chance to place their families under better conditions and to win a larger life than the life that they had left behind. He who believes that even the hordes of recent immigrants from southern Italy are drawn to these shores by nothing more than a dull and blind materialism has not penetrated into the heart of the problem. The idealism and expectation of these children of the Old World, the hopes which they have formed for a newer and freer life across the seas, are almost pathetic when one considers how far they are from the possibility of fruition. He who would take stock of American democracy must not forget the accumulation of human purposes and ideals which immigration has added to the American populace.

In this connection it must also be remembered that these democratic ideals have existed at each stage of the advance of the frontier, and have left behind them deep and enduring effects on the thinking of the whole country. Long after the frontier period of a particular region of the United States has passed away, the conception of society, the ideals and aspirations which it produced, persist in the minds of the people. So recent has been the transition of the greater portion of the United States from frontier conditions to conditions of settled life, that we are, over the large portion of the United States, hardly a generation removed from the primitive conditions of the West. If, indeed, we ourselves were not pioneers, our fathers were, and the inherited ways of looking at things, the fundamental assumptions of the American people, have all been shaped by this experience of democracy on its westward march. This experience has been wrought into the very warp and woof of American thought.

Even those masters of industry and capital who have risen to power by the conquest of Western resources came from the midst of this society and still profess its principles. John D. Rockefeller was born on a New York farm, and began his career as a young business man in St. Louis. Marcus Hanna was a Cleveland grocer's clerk at the age of twenty. Claus Spreckles, the sugar king, came from Germany as a steerage passenger to the United States in 1848. Marshall Field was a farmer boy in Conway, Massachusetts, until he left to grow up with the young Chicago. Andrew Carnegie came as a ten-year-old boy from Scotland to Pittsburgh, then a distinctively Western town. He built up his fortunes through successive grades until he became the dominating factor in the great iron industries, and paved the way for that colossal achievement, the Steel Trust. Whatever may be the tendencies of this corporation, there can be little doubt of the democratic ideals of Mr. Carnegie himself. With lavish hand he has strewn millions through the United States for the promotion of libraries. The effect of this library movement in perpetuating the democracy that comes from an intelligent and self-respecting people can hardly be measured. In his "Triumphant Democracy," published in 1886, Mr. Carnegie, the ironmaster, said in reference to the mineral wealth of the United States: "Thank God, these treasures are in the hands of an intelligent people, the Democracy, to be used for the general good of the masses, and not made the spoils of monarchs, courts, and aristoc-

racy, to be turned to the base and selfish ends of a privileged hereditary class." It would be hard to find a more rigorous assertion of democratic doctrine than the celebrated utterance, attributed to the same man, that he should feel it a disgrace to die rich.

In enumerating the services of American democracy, President Eliot included the corporation as one of its achievements, declaring that "freedom of incorporation, though no longer exclusively a democratic agency, has given a strong support to democratic institutions." In one sense this is doubtless true, since the corporation has been one of the means by which small properties can be aggregated into an effective working body. Socialistic writers have long been fond of pointing out also that these various concentrations pave the way for and make possible social control. From this point of view it is possible that the masters of industry may prove to be not so much an incipient aristocracy as the pathfinders for democracy in reducing the industrial world to systematic consolidation suited to democratic control. The great geniuses that have built up the modern industrial concentration were trained in the midst of democratic society. They were the product of these democratic conditions. Freedom to rise was the very condition of their existence. Whether they will be followed by successors who will adopt the exploitation of the masses, and who will be capable of retaining under efficient control these vast resources, is one of the questions which we shall have to face.

This, at least, is clear: American democracy is fundamentally the outcome of the experiences of the American people in dealing with the West. Western democracy through the whole of its earlier period tended to the production of a society of which the most distinctive fact was the freedom of the individual to rise under conditions of social mobility, and whose ambition was the liberty and well-being of the masses. This conception has vitalized all American democracy, and has brought it into sharp contrasts with the democracies of history, and with those modern efforts of Europe to create an artificial democratic order by legislation. The problem of the United States is not to create democracy, but to conserve democratic institutions and ideals. In the later period of its development, Western democracy has been gaining experience in the problem of social control. It has steadily enlarged the sphere of its action and the instruments for its perpetuation. By its system of public schools, from the grades to the graduate work of the great universities, the West has created a larger single body of intelligent plain people than can be found elsewhere in the world. Its political tendencies, whether we consider Democracy, Populism, or Republicanism, are distinctly in the direction of greater social control and the conservation of the old democratic ideals.

To these ideals the West adheres with even a passionate determination. If, in working out its mastery of the resources of the interior, it has produced a type of industrial leader so powerful as to be the wonder of the world, nevertheless, it is still to be determined whether these men constitute a menace to democratic institutions, or the most efficient factor for adjusting democratic control to the new conditions.

Whatever shall be the outcome of the rush of this huge industrial modern United States to its place among the nations of the earth, the formation of its Western democracy will always remain one of the wonderful chapters in the history of the human race. Into this vast shaggy continent of ours poured the first feeble tide of European settlement. European men, institutions, and ideas were lodged in the American wilderness, and this great American West took them to her bosom, taught them a new way of looking upon the destiny of the common man, trained them in adaptation to the conditions of the New World, to the creation of new institutions to meet new needs; and ever as society on her eastern border grew to resemble the Old World in its social forms and its industry, ever as it began to lose faith in the ideals of democracy, she opened new provinces, and dowered new democracies in her most distant domains with her material treasures and with the ennobling influence that the fierce love of freedom, the strength that came from hewing out a home, making a school and a church, and creating a higher future for his family, furnished to the pioneer.

She gave to the world such types as the farmer Thomas Jefferson, with his Declaration of Independence, his statute for religious toleration, and his purchase of Louisiana. She gave us Andrew Jackson, that fierce Tennessee spirit who broke down the traditions of conservative rule, swept away the privacies and privileges of officialdom, and, like a Gothic leader, opened the temple of the nation to the populace. She gave us Abraham Lincoln, whose gaunt frontier form and gnarled, massive hand told of the conflict with the forest, whose grasp of the ax-handle of the pioneer was no firmer than his grasp of the helm of the ship of state as it breasted the seas of civil war. She has furnished to this new democracy her stores of mineral wealth, that dwarf those of the Old World, and her provinces that in themselves are vaster and more productive than most of the nations of Europe. Out of her bounty has come a nation whose industrial competition alarms the Old World, and the masters of whose resources wield wealth and power vaster than the wealth and power of kings. Best of all, the West gave, not only to the American, but to the unhappy and oppressed of all lands, a vision of hope, and assurance that the world held a place where were to be found high faith in man and the will and power to furnish him the opportunity to grow to the full measure of his own capacity. Great and powerful as are the new sons of her loins, the Republic is greater than they. The paths of the pioneer have widened into broad highways. The forest clearing has expanded into affluent commonwealths. Let us see to it that the ideals of the pioneer in his log cabin shall enlarge into the spiritual life of a democracy where civic power shall dominate and utilize individual achievement for the common good.

Benjamin F. Wright, Jr.:

POLITICAL INSTITUTIONS AND THE FRONTIER

IN this essay on the early development of political systems in the Middle West I have two objectives. I desire, first, to trace some of the principal lines of institutional growth because of their significance in the constitutional history of the United States. That portion of our history is much more than the story of the national constitution and its interpretation. In any political society, and particularly in one organized on the federal principle, the development of local institutions is an essential part of the entire pattern; in some respects and at certain periods it is of more consequence in the lives of the citizens of the country than the changes which may be taking place in the central structure. The westward migration of constitutional customs surely deserves a more careful analytical and comparative study than it has yet received. Second, I wish to use the material brought together for this purpose as a point of departure from which to appraise the interpretation of American history first propounded by Frederick Jackson Turner forty years ago. The most brilliant and the most influential of American historians, Turner has colored all of our thinking about the growth of the American nation. His striking generalizations have been repeated countless times, but they have never been subjected either to the analysis or to the tests which the rudiments of scientific method would seem to suggest. A picture of the movement of political institutions is not one of sufficient scope to make possible a complete consideration of so inclusive a thesis. Indeed the whole canvas of American history is inadequate for the purpose; one must in addition take into account many aspects of Canadian, Latin American, and European history. But if a complete re-examination is neither possible nor intended here, a partial consideration may at least suggest the principal points of strength and of weakness in the frontier approach.

In dealing with the constitutional beginnings of the Middle West I shall concern myself not with the very earliest political society of that region but with its institutions when they are first embodied in written constitutions and relatively settled laws. There are, aside from limits of space, three reasons for doing so. In the first place, the earliest institutions, so far as they were sufficiently established to be dignified with that name, were frequently temporary expedients designed to serve a temporary purpose. They were intended for the period in which of necessity the pioneers concentrated upon essentials. In the second place, the settlers of the territorial period were not entirely free agents. The Ordinance for the Northwest Territory was one of the most liberal statutes ever enacted for the government of a territory, but it did determine many aspects of early political activity. Finally, and most important, is the reason that the real test of the frontier period's influence is not the history of that short period but the history of what resulted when the pioneers left it behind and adopted for themselves institutions of their own choosing. It is here that we have the opportunity to estimate the results of the period of primitive existence through which the frontiersman had lived.

So far as I have been able to determine, there was no considerable desire among those who framed the early western constitutions to introduce governmental forms different from those long well established in the East. In all of the states of the Middle West the familiar pattern was adopted, — a single executive, a bicameral legislature, and a hierarchy of courts. The only exception to this system in any new state was Vermont, and its unicameral legislative system was a direct copy of that contained in the Pennsylvania constitution of 1776. The abandonment of this provision in 1836 brought to an end an experiment which might have had considerable value.

In local government the story is much the same, excepting that here there were somewhat greater variations among the sections of the East. The result, in general, was a parallel westward movement of local institutions. To be sure, the scattered character of western settlement, together with the artificial township boundaries of that area, prevented the

settlers from New England from establishing a thoroughgoing New England town system, but otherwise there is no important exception to the principle of westward extension of local forms. In Ohio, for example, a county-township system upon the Pennsylvania model was established, and subsequently copied in Indiana. Michigan, probably because of a relatively larger migration from New York following the opening of the Erie Canal, adopted the township-county system of that state, one in which the township played a somewhat greater role in local affairs and in which the county board was composed of township supervisors. This was later copied in Wisconsin. In early Illinois, because of heavy immigration from the South, the county was of more importance than in other states of the section. As the northern part of the state grew in population and influence, the desire for the township system developed. In consequence the constitution of 1848 made that form, on the New York-Michigan model, optional, and it was subsequently adopted in most of the northern counties while those in the southern part of the state continued under the former system.

As urban areas developed in these states, the forms of municipal government found in the older states were introduced. Even the cumbersome bicameral municipal council crossed the Alleghenies and found a home (fortunately temporary) in the new cities.

Probably the most characteristic political idea of the American people is distrust of elected officers, legislative and executive. Certainly in this country we have hedged their powers about more carefully than has any other democracy. This distrust is manifested in the detailed character of our constitutions, in the difficulty of amending them, in the principle of separation of powers with its correlative, checks and balances, and in judicial review of legislative and executive actions.

So far as concerns the length and scope of their constitutions, the middle western states differed not at all from contemporaneous eastern models. During the Revolution the tendency was toward longer and more detailed documents, as a comparison of the Massachusetts constitution of 1780 with those adopted in 1776 will show. That tendency has continued to our own time. The Illinois constitution of 1848, for example, is over twice as long as that of 1818. And although there is perfectly definite evidence in the earlier document of something less than complete trust in the legislature and governor, that distrust had grown to such an extent by 1848 that many questions earlier left to be determined by those departments were now regulated by constitutional provision.

In six of the Revolutionary constitutions there was a distributing clause, that is, a clause stating the separation of powers principle, and specifying that it should be observed in the government established under that constitution. In most of those documents there was, by later standards, little separation between legislature and governor. But it is evident that there was a strong tendency in that direction, as the New York constitution of 1777, in which the governor was made elective by the people rather than by the legislature, and the Massachusetts constitution of 1780 indicate. The second constitutions of New Hampshire (1784), Pennsylvania (1790), and Delaware (1792) reflect the strength of this tendency. It was the lead of these states which was followed in the Old Northwest. And in all of the early constitutions of this region save those of

Ohio and Wisconsin, there was a distributing clause. In those states the national constitution, which separates even its statement of the separation principle, was the model.

Ohio, in its first constitution, followed the example of most of the Revolutionary constitutions in giving to the governor no veto. Illinois first adopted the New York system of bestowing this power upon a council of revision, made up of the governor and certain of the judges. All of the other states adopted a variant of the executive veto which had previously been adopted in Massachusetts, in the national constitution and in the second or third constitutions of a number of eastern states. In one respect, however, most of them followed the lead of Kentucky. In the first constitution of that state the Massachusetts-national system according to which the executive veto could be overridden by a two-thirds vote of both houses was adopted, but in its second constitution (1799) it reduced the vote required to a majority of the total membership of both houses. The popularity of this system in the West would seem to indicate that the governor was not so generally hailed as the trusted man of the people as has sometimes been supposed. Its later abandonment by all except one or two of the states indicates that it was not to be an innovation of lasting importance.

The item veto, one of the most powerful weapons the governor now has, was first introduced by New Jersey in 1844 and was subsequently copied in many western constitutions.

Judicial review is a conservative device which no other country in the world has imitated, excepting to the extent that the courts serve as referee between central governments and member states in a number of federal systems. It developed here in the colonial and early constitutional periods out of a variety of circumstances and ideas. So far as I have been able to determine, no American constitution has made provision for it, but during the late eighteenth and early nineteenth centuries its use became general, in the West as in the East.

What has been said about the structure and relative powers of the departments of government applies with equal force to the tenure of office. In the original constitutions there was a strong tendency toward annual elections, but there was also very considerable variation. The western states ordinarily chose neither the briefest nor the longest tenures, although sometimes they did both in the same constitution, but were somewhere between the extremes. In general, there is no indication in this regard of any genuine difference between the opinions of contemporaneous constitution makers, in the older and in the newer states.

There remain to be considered those institutions which have an even more direct bearing than do the ones thus far considered upon the extent to which the political society of this section reflected a desire for a broader distribution of power and privilege, that is, for greater democracy.

The pioneers took over, without question, the device of a written constitution as the expressed will of the people. They further imitated one or another of the plans for the preparation, adoption, and amendment of such documents. When the Massachusetts convention in 1778 submitted to the voters a proposed constitution it was inaugurating the democratic method which was, sooner or later, to be followed by almost every state in the union. The method provided for the revision of the constitution in that state, by a convention elected for the purpose

after the voters had expressed their desire for such action, or that adopted in Maryland in 1776, a favorable vote in two successive legislatures, was the pattern followed in all of the western states.

All of the early western constitutions, furthermore, contained bills of rights. The models here were, of course, the Revolutionary constitutions, certain provisions of the Ordinance for the Northwest Territory, and the relevant parts of the Constitution of the United States. The new states occasionally made a few additions to the conventional list of reserved rights, but, without exception, they represented no genuine change in political ideals or constitutional practice.

Perhaps the most frequent claim made for the democratizing influence of the pioneer period is the lead taken by the states which passed through this phase during the late eighteenth and early nineteenth centuries in securing a broader suffrage. That these new states did help to accelerate a process under way before they were settled is clear. But it is equally clear that they did not attempt, or even desire, to carry that process beyond the goal previously attained in several of the older states. The broadening of the suffrage really began during the Revolution when five states measurably reduced the amount of the property required. One state, Pennsylvania, went beyond this and imposed no property requirement other than the payment of some public tax. By 1792 four other states, South Carolina, New Hampshire, Georgia, and Delaware, had followed Pennsylvania's example. Two of these, New Hampshire and Georgia, abandoned even the tax qualification by 1798, but when Ohio entered the union in 1802 her constitution contained that limitation. It was not until 1816, when Indiana became a state, that any state in what is now the Middle West went further than had Pennsylvania in 1776, and by that time not only New Hampshire and Georgia, but also Maryland and South Carolina, had dropped both property and tax qualifications. Indiana and the other states of this section which followed her example were not blazing a new trail; they were proceeding along one clearly marked for them by the more advanced states of the East. They showed no intention of pushing that path further. Indeed, all of them excluded free Negroes, although New York and five of the New England states admitted them to the suffrage right.

The influence of the newer states upon the reduction of the qualifications for the holding of legislative and executive offices is similar to, but probably greater than, their influence upon the suffrage. In nearly all of the older states property qualifications for office holding continued into the nineteenth century. In a few of them religious qualifications are also to be found. That these limitations would not long have survived the forces that had for decades, perhaps for centuries, been at work in the eastern part of the United States and in the western part of Europe is hardly to be questioned. Nevertheless it does seem to be clear that the newer western states, which, excepting for two or three in the lower Mississippi area, adopted neither property nor religious qualifications upon office holding, helped to speed up the process of democratizing that part of the constitutional system.

We have frequently been told that it was the pioneer regions in such states as Virginia and South Carolina which struggled for and finally secured something approximating representation on a population basis in the legislatures. One could wish for a more inclusive account here,

for in many states, especially in New England, the process is almost reversed. Long before any western state was admitted to the union we find in eastern constitutions the statement of the principle of representation according to population. Vested interests in those states sometimes prevented the application of this rule with complete impartiality. In the earlier period it was usually the thinly settled areas which were discriminated against, but later it was the rural sections which, in states east and west, prevented the cities from having their proportionate share of representatives. One of the most striking examples of this is the long refusal of the Illinois legislature to redistribute seats in that body so that Cook County might be represented in accordance with its increased population.

In the number of executive and judicial officers elected by popular vote the influence of the western states is more definitely to be seen. As I have previously pointed out, there was during the last quarter of the eighteenth century a marked tendency toward the elective governorship. The same tendency is found in the case of the lieutenant-governorship and in that of the total membership of the legislature. The older states provided, however, that the other state executive and judicial officers, excepting for some holding positions of local jurisdiction, should be appointed by the governor or by the legislature. In all of the constitutions adopted in the Middle West before 1848 the example of the eastern states is followed. There were relatively few new constitutions adopted in the East during the first half of the nineteenth century, but in those the practice of popular election for officers other than the governor and the legislators made slow headway. Connecticut in 1818 did provide for popular election of a treasurer and secretary, but this was exceptional. The first state to adopt a constitution requiring the election of virtually all of the judicial and executive officers of the state was Mississippi, which did so not in its first constitution of 1817, but in the second constitution which came fifteen years later. The example of this state was not followed by Michigan when it framed its first constitution in 1835, nor by Iowa in 1846, but after the acceptance of the general elective principle by Illinois and Wisconsin in 1848 the older methods of appointment were soon abandoned in most of the other states.

Because the eastern states had in many instances provided for popular election of local officials there was less opportunity for the western constitutions to introduce a broadened electoral system for county and townships than for state governments. With a few exceptions and some slight modifications they simply followed the example of the more democratic eastern systems.

If the material on the early constitutional history of the Middle West has been accurately stated, the following set of conclusions would appear to be justified:

In their choice of political institutions the men of this section were imitative, not creative. They were not interested in making experiments. Their constitutional, like their domestic, architecture was patterned after that of the communities from which they had moved westward. However different their life during the period of frontier existence may have been from that of the older communities, they showed no substantial desire to retain its primitive characteristics when they established laws and constitutions of their own choice. To be sure

they ordinarily, although not invariably, adopted the more democratic practices where there was variation in the East, but even in this respect they never varied from some well-established seaboard model, unless it was in the case of the proportion of elected officials. And even in this instance, which came not directly from the pioneering period but after a considerable interval had elapsed, one can trace precedents and some tendencies in this direction in the older states. In short, the result of the developments in the newer section seems to have been somewhat to accelerate the rate of growth of the democratic movement, not to change its direction.

It will be remembered that in his original essay on the influence of the frontier Turner wrote in the crusading mood of one who battles for a dear and a long-neglected cause. It was with vigor and enthusiasm that "he hitched his star to a covered wagon." His conclusions begin with his first paragraph and they lack not in inclusiveness. "The existence of an area of free land, its continuous recession, and the advance of American settlement westward, explain American development. . . . The true point of view in the history of this nation is not the Atlantic coast, it is the Great West."[1] Like most historians of his time he believed individualistic American democracy to be the fine flower of modern civilization. And it, along with the other characteristic features of American life, could be accounted for only by reference to the frontier.[2] The principal arguments supporting this conclusion seem to be the democratic character of pioneer life, the effect of free land upon the discontented and the ambitious and the

[1] Turner, *The Frontier in American History*, pp. 1, 3.

[2] *Ibid.*, pp. 30 ff.

opposition of the frontiersmen to unjust control by the dwellers in the eastern communities. In many essays written during the next ten years the changes are rung on these early assertions. And the cynic who said that "history may not repeat itself but historians repeat each other" was something of a prophet so far as Turner's numerous followers are concerned. Reiteration of Turner's generalizations, or, more often, the implicit assumption of their truth, has been their scholarly method of testifying to his influence. I have elsewhere argued that the frontier interpretation is inadequate, even seriously misleading, as an explanation for the growth of American democracy.[3] I wish here merely to consider the applicability of one part of this body of doctrine to the early constitutional development of the Middle West.

In an article published in 1896 and dealing with the attempts at state-making by the Westerners during the Revolution, this statement appears in the conclusions: "The frontier modified older forms and infused into them the spirit of democracy."[4] Later in the same year came an essay in which he said that: "The history of our political institutions, our democracy, is not a history of imitation, of simple borrowing; it is a history of the evolution and adaptation of organs in response to changed environment, a history of the origin of new political species. In this sense, therefore, the West has been a constructive force of the highest significance in our life."[5] And, on the next page, "This forest philosophy is the philosophy of American democracy." Many similar statements dot the essays published during the next twenty years or more. A quotation from

one published in 1914 may serve to illustrate the point of view so frequently restated. "Their [the pioneers'] most fundamental traits, their institutions, even their ideals were shaped by this interaction between the wilderness and themselves."[6] Even in the preface to the volume of essays published in 1920 appears a characteristic reference to the "transforming influence of the American wilderness."

Now it is, of course, true that during the period of genuinely frontier existence the folkways, the institutions, of the pioneers were necessarily adjusted to the exigencies of primitive living. But where is the evidence that the experiences of such a period resulted in the re-shaping of the institutions of American democracy? The frontier era was ordinarily one of short duration. If my interpretation of the data is correct, those who had lived through such a time were at least as desirous of establishing political and legal systems on the eastern model as they had been when they moved to the frontier. Of course, since most of them were men who, in the older states, were among the under-privileged, they usually desired to adopt the constitutional devices which gave to more persons a share in political power. But as they showed no desire to tinker with the institution of property or to allow their legislatures to pass laws violating the sanctity of contracts, so too they did not extend political powers to women or to Negroes. I may perhaps add that my own observations of the institutional life of a state removed by only a few decades from the time of the frontiersmen strengthen my belief that the conception of the "transforming influence" of the frontier, as it appears in Turner's essays, is largely a myth. Indeed, I believe that a much better argument can

[3] "American Democracy and the Frontier," *Yale Review*, XX (1930), 349.
[4] Turner, *Sections in American History*, p. 136.
[5] *The Frontier in American History*, pp. 205–206.
[6] *Ibid.*, p. 293.

be made out that the hardships of pioneer living transformed a large proportion of the restless and discontented who
migrated to the free and promised lands
into men ambitious to be prosperous citizens in the image of the bankers and
merchants and landowners back home.
If this thesis isn't always applicable to
some of the wilder and farther West, it
is eminently so to the Middle West.

That reference to some of the differences between various "Wests" gives an
opportunity to introduce a penultimate
observation. The so-called frontier interpretation was never simply that. Among
other things it was, from the beginning,
a sectional interpretation of American
history.[7] A glance at the titles as well
as an analysis of the content in *The
Frontier in American History* indicates
as much. Furthermore, it is in good part
a Middle West-sectional interpretation.
A devoted citizen of that region, Turner
almost invariably had its history and its
characteristics in mind when he generalized about the West or the frontier. Con-
sequently an analysis of the influence of
the frontier upon the political development of the Middle West is particularly
favorable to the Turner thesis. In the
South West, for example, slavery was not
the only undemocratic institution carried from the old to the new lands. And
if I could choose for my point of reference the Great Salt Lake Basin it would
be easy to prove that frontier life transformed those who had lived under a
comparatively individualistic and democratic system into the loyal adherents of
oligarchy and paternalism. Doubtless it
also accounts for the change from mo-
nogamy to polygamy.

There is one final, possibly fatal, challenge to deal with. The usual answer to

any criticism of Turner's doctrine is
about this: "Turner never said what you
make him say. You have only set up a
man of straw and then proceeded to de-
molish him." I think that the difficulty
of interpretation here is largely due to
the two-fold character of Turner's work.
He was both a remarkably able investigator of relatively detailed points of historical scholarship and a poet who wrote
in the grand manner. As a teacher he
was cautious in the extreme. His acuteness as a researcher was equaled by his
hesitancy in formulating broad conclusions. But in his poetic capacity he wrote
brilliant and moving odes to the glories
of the westward movement. In 1893 he
stated his propositions not as hypothesis
but as thesis. During the next twenty-
five years he published the twelve essays
included along with the original one in
the *Frontier* volume. They contain elab-
orations of the original doctrine, but they
do not contain qualifications nor any expression of doubt as to the complete truth
of the original declarations. The statements from his writings which I quoted
were wrested from the context and
doubtless they appear somewhat less extreme when read in the light of the complete argument. But such statements are
made and repeated so frequently that
they are not exceptional, and certainly
they are never qualified. Some of the
most romantic passages appear in essays
written toward the close of Turner's career. Consider, for example, the well-
known paragraph in the essay published
in 1914, twenty-one years after the first
essay appeared: "American democracy
was born of no theorist's dream; it was
not carried in the *Susan Constant* to Virginia nor in the *Mayflower* to Plymouth.
It came out of the American forest, and
it gained new strength each time it
touched a new frontier. Not the constitution, but free land and an abundance

[7] I have commented upon this characteristic of
Turner's writings in a review of his *Sections*. See
The New England Quarterly, VI (1933), 630.

of natural resources open to a fit people, made the democratic type of society in America for three centuries while it occupied its empire."[8]

As an exhortation to the faithful, a colorful declaration of American independence from European ideas and practices, and a fine tribute to those of our ancestors who carved for us homes and security out of the wilderness, it is a splendid piece of writing. But, unfortunately, it is more misleading than it is helpful. Let us consider it briefly.

If any one ever said that American democracy was the product of a single theorist's dreams, or, for that matter, the product of the entire residuum of political speculation, he probably was not taken very seriously. Obviously no theorist or group of theorists dreamed into existence the queer patchwork of institutions that we call American democracy. But what is gained, except misunderstanding, by an ungracious exclusion of Locke and Milton and Montesquieu, of Coke and Blackstone and Grotius, of Adams, Jefferson, Otis, Paine, and Madison from a share of the credit? One has but to compare the differences between the institutions of the English and those of the French, Dutch, and Spanish colonies in America to see that the foundations, and more, of our democracy were brought in the *Susan Constant* and *Mayflower*. That democracy did not come out of the American forest unless it was first carried there. On some frontiers democracy was not strengthened, rather the reverse. Free land gave the opportunity to establish slavery in Louisiana, oligarchy in the Mormon state, the hacienda system in Mexican California, while it was furnishing the opportunity for a "fit" people in the Middle West to establish the par-

8 *The Frontier in American History*, p. 293.

ticular degree and kind of democracy that they favored.

If Turner's thesis had not been so widely relied upon, there would be no point at this late date in subjecting his generalizations to critical analysis. Certainly I have no desire to disparage his standing as an historian nor to minimize the stimulating effect that his writings had upon the American historiography of the last generation. He did have the genius to see in certain neglected factors extraordinarily useful instruments. If, in his zeal for his cause, he over-stated his case, that was more than pardonable, it was probably necessary. But the desirability of unquestioning acceptance of his sweeping doctrine vanished long ago. His thesis has, like previous interpretations, served its purpose. Continued reliance upon his unclarified and unmodified doctrine is more an indication of imaginative poverty than of loyalty to a dead leader. It has been many times said that each generation must reinterpret history to suit its own preconceptions. If we to-day find Turner's thesis of forty years ago to have been narrow and provincial, to have emphasized unduly the characteristics peculiar to some sections and some frontiers, to have elevated to the stature of universal principles values which are beginning to be found something less than perfect, we are simply doing for our time what he did for his. And the longer such an attitude is postponed, the more likely is it that instead of critical appraisal, which would mean the retention of the still useful portions of Turner's thesis as well as the discarding of those found to have outlived their time, we shall have uncompromising attack in which the destruction might be spectacular but the salvage negligible.

Louis M. Hacker: SECTIONS — OR CLASSES?

FREDERICK Jackson Turner was thirty-two years old in 1893 when he read his monograph, "The Significance of the Frontier in American History," before the American Historical Association. From that day, forty years ago, until now it may truly be said that he has so completely dominated American historical writing that hardly a single production in all that time has failed to show the marks of his influence. Not only were Turner's own seminar students legion (he taught altogether for some thirty-four years) but his personal followers in turn scattered over the land to indoctrinate other vast numbers of eager scholars, thereby increasing the Turner host by geometric proportions. All these disciples, whether of the first, second, or third degree, were historians as well as teachers; the result has been the accumulation of a vast pile of monographic studies and special investigations, all of them concerned with aspects of the settlement and institutional development of the American West. So intensively have all these persons labored, so closely have they covered the field of American history with the fine web of their researches, that one scarcely exaggerates in saying that the patient and obscure toiling of another long generation of American historical scholars will be required to destroy this influence: for Turner and his followers were the fabricators of a tra-

dition which is not only fictitious but also to a very large extent positively harmful.

Turner's own contributions to American historical literature were modest. He wrote one volume for the American Nation Series called "The Rise of the New West" (a history of the United States from 1820 to 1830), which was published in 1906; he was engaged when he died in 1932 on another work that was to continue the story to 1850; and he was responsible for not more than some thirty learned essays and general articles. The more representative of these have been collected in two volumes: the first, entitled "The Frontier in American History," was published in 1920; the second is the subject of this review.

The Turner thesis, which is not proved so much as it is continually reiterated in the papers of the two volumes of collected essays, may be summed up as follows: American development was unique in historical annals in that it was constantly being conditioned by the series of frontier zones which succeeded each other until the year 1890; and what made the frontier an ever-present force in American history was the existence of vast reaches of free arable lands. Into these successions of Western areas poured waves of pioneering spirits to influence, subtly but pervasively, all forms of American living. Particularly, these were the outstanding effects of the fron-

This review of Turner's *The Significance of Sections in American History* is reprinted from the *Nation*, 137 (July 26, 1933), 108–110, by permission of the author and the publisher.

tier: out of the common experiences of the Western zones emerged a distinctly American people; under the cruel conditions of frontier pioneering, where only the hardy individual could survive, was born the doctrine of democracy; because the frontier areas were in effect creations of the American government and because the frontiersmen looked to Washington for comfort and relief, loyalty was to the nation and not to the individual States — hence the American nationalistic spirit; and finally, because the Westerners regarded their governments not as sovereign controllers but as agencies for the performance of delegated public functions, the frontier States were turned into so many social laboratories where experiments in the extension of public activities were continually going on. Such were the peculiar contributions made by the presence of the frontier to America's development and progress; these were to be the subjects for scholarly inquiry.

So much for American civilization during its dynamic phases when its history was the conquest of a series of wilderness environments. But what of subsequent periods? The United States would then become "a settled nation" and reach "a more stable equilibrium" in which the chief influence at work, again differentiating American civilization from all others, would be the existence of sections. In these sections, formed by "physiographic conditions, economic interests, and constituent stocks of settled societies," where denser populations would be pressing upon the means of subsistence, would spring up groups of peoples as unlike each other as the different nations of Europe. In 1925 Turner therefore wrote: "The significant fact is that sectional self-consciousness and sensitiveness is likely to be increased as time goes on and crystallized sections feel the full influence of their geographic peculiarities, their special interests, and their developed ideals, in a closed and static nation." And in the same paper he could coolly declare: "Economic interests are sectionalized."

The analogy between the United States as a "congeries of sections" and Europe as a collection of nations particularly fascinated Turner, for he returned to it again and again. The American "physical map may be regarded as a map of potential nations and empires," he said in 1904; and the American section "is the faint image of a European nation," he repeated as late as 1925. Indeed, Europe had much to learn from American experiences: if a United States of America could be erected, why not a United States of Europe, where, too, "by substituting discussion and concession and compromised legislation for force," there could also be achieved "international political parties, international legislative bodies, and international peace"? The histories, interests, ideals, cultural achievements of American sections, then, were to be the second great field for research.

In 1922, now assuming the role of prophet in place of the customary one of preceptor, Turner, by drawing upon both his frontier and sectional hypotheses, indicated what the future of the United States was to be:

However profound the economic changes, we shall not give up our American ideals and our hopes for men, which had their origin in our own pioneering experience, in favor of any mechanical solution offered by doctrinaires educated in Old World grievances. Rather, we shall find strength to build from our past a nobler structure, in which each section will find its place as a fit room in a worthy house.

A detailed examination of the amazing errors into which Turner fell in order to prove his two assumptions of the uniqueness of the frontier experience and the continuity of sectional differences is hardly necessary even if space permitted. Merely to mention these rather naive ideas as I have is enough to confute them. Nor am I particularly concerned with the many evidences of historical ignorance that Turner's papers in both volumes of collected miscellany on every hand display: his statement for example in an article in 1924 that American exports of foodstuffs to Europe were "directly influential upon Bismarck's policy of tariffs, state socialism, colonial empire, and sea power"; or his remark first made in 1904 and again repeated in 1925 that the Civil War's form and "its causes were fundamentally shaped by the dynamic factor of expanding sections, of a West to be won"; or his characterization in 1924 of American radical labor as being made up of "chiefly recent aliens, who interpret America in terms of Russia and adopt the policy of syndicalism."

What is of greater concern is the perverted reading Turner gave to American history in his insistence upon the uniqueness of American experience and his emphasis upon sectional development as a sort of flywheel to balance all political, social, and economic disparities. The unhappy results, for forty years, were the following: a turning inward of American historical activity at exactly the time when all trained eyes should have been on events going on beyond the country's physical borders; an accumulation of supposed evidences of the development of American institutions entirely in nativistic terms without an understanding of how closely American institutional growth paralleled the European; an almost complete disregard of the basic class antagonisms in American history; and a profound ignorance of the steps by which monopolistic capitalism and imperialism were being developed in the

country. Granted that with the aid of the Turner hypotheses many interesting historical works were written: examinations of the shaping of the country's land policy, the Middle West's settlement by New England, the building of the railroads, the rise and fall of the cow country, the creation of Western farmers' organizations, and the like; can one doubt in the light of Turner's own definition of the function of historical research — "it is important to study the present and recent past, not only for themselves but also as the source of new hypotheses, new lines of inquiry, new criteria of the perspective of the remoter past" — that this extraordinary collection of learning is quite worthless?

Had Turner not so boldly cut himself loose from the currents of European thought which his teachers at Johns Hopkins were trying to emphasize through their talk of "the continuity of history" and the "inheritance of institutions," had he given more attention to the activities of some of his contemporaries instead of to the Wisconsin fur trade (the subject of his doctoral thesis) — for example, to H. D. Lloyd's "Wealth Against Commonwealth" which was published in 1890 and which gave a complete exposition of the steps by which monopolistic capitalism was being attained, or to A. T. Mahon's "The United States Looking Outward," also published in 1890, which on the basis of sound premises predicted an imperialistic career for the United States — then our own past, in the light of America's current needs, might not be the sealed book it is today.

Turner undoubtedly was right in pointing out the significance that free lands played in American development. The free lands of the West were not important, however, because they made possible the creation of a unique "American spirit" — that indefinable something that was to set the United States apart from European experiences for all time — but because their quick settlement and utilization for the extensive cultivation of foodstuffs furnished exactly those commodities with which the United States, as a debtor nation, could balance its international payments and borrow European capital in order to develop a native industrial enterprise. Thus, in the first place, agriculture, primarily the agriculture of those Western areas of which Turner made so much, was really a catspaw for industry; once having served its purpose, that is to say the capitalist development of the nation, it could be neglected politically and ultimately abandoned economically. In the second place, the presence of the frontier helps to explain the failure of American labor to preserve a continuous revolutionary tradition: class lines could not become fixed as long as the free lands existed to drain off the most spirited elements in the working and lower middle-class populations — not only as farmers, of course, but as small merchants and enterprisers, too — and to prevent the creation of a labor reserve for the purpose of thwarting the demands of organized workers.

The historical growth of the United States, in short, was not unique; merely in certain particulars and for a brief time, it was different from the European pattern largely because of the processes of settlement. With settlement achieved — that is to say, the historic function of extensive agriculture performed, class (not sectional!) lines solidified, competitive capitalism converted into monopolistic capitalism under the guidance of the money power, and imperialism the ultimate destiny of the nation — the United States once again was returning to the main stream of European institutional development. Only by a study of the origins and growth of American capitalism and imperialism can we obtain insight into the nature and complexity of the problems confronting us today. And I am prepared to submit that perhaps the chief reason for the absence of this proper understanding was the futile hunt for a unique "American spirit" which Frederick Jackson Turner began forty years ago and in which he involved most of America's historical scholars from that time until now.

George Wilson Pierson:

THE FRONTIER AND
AMERICAN INSTITUTIONS
A Criticism of the Turner Theory

HOW much of Frederick Jackson Turner's frontier hypothesis is reliable and useful today? This problem has begun to trouble economists, sociologists, geographers, and most of all the teachers of graduate students in the field of American history.

For how shall we account for the industrial revolution by the frontier? Do American music and architecture come from the woods? Did American cattle? Were our religions born of the contemplation of untamed nature? Has science, poetry, or even democracy, its cradle in the wilderness? Did literature grow fertile with innovation in the open spaces? Above all, what happens to intellectual history if the environment be all?

The predicament of the scholar, who has been living in a comfortable frontier philosophy, is beginning to attract some attention. Nor may we comfort ourselves with the assurance that ours is a purely academic debate. For frontier legends of one kind or another have now so permeated American thought as to threaten drastic consequences. Have not our most influential journalists and statesmen for some time been ringing *pessimistic* changes on the theme of "lost frontier," "lost safety-valve," "lost opportunity"?[1] Such convictions can lead to legislation. In Congress the underlying issue could shortly be: was there but one economic frontier, was it really a "safety-valve," and are both now gone? The cultural historian meanwhile asks: is it true that the frontier was "the line of most rapid and effective Americanization"? More particularly, since we are now trying to define and safeguard the "American way of life," what share did the "frontier" have in its creation, and to what cultural influences must we henceforth look for its preservation?

No matter how phrased, these questions are fundamental. They suggest a serious re-study of our premises. And the

[1] Recently, at Union College, President Dixon Ryan Fox pointed out how the Turner doctrine has tended to encourage defeatism during the last decade. Too many prophets have argued that the disappearance of free frontier land means the disappearance of opportunity. On the contrary, said President Fox, the word frontier ought to mean merely "the edge of the unused." In science, in business, in arts, challenge remains. "A failure now . . . would not be a failure of opportunity; it would be a failure of nerve."

I am indebted to President Fox for permission to quote from his address, and for some most pertinent suggestions; also, for criticism and encouragement to Charles A. Beard, to Professors Leonard W. Labaree and James G. Leyburn of Yale University, and to Professor Richard H. Shryock of the University of Pennsylvania.

From the *New England Quarterly*, 15 (June, 1942), 224–255, by permission of the publisher.

place to begin, the present writer has concluded, is with Professor Turner's own theories in the matter: that is, with his celebrated and influential essays on the significance of the American frontier.[2]

My proposal is, therefore, first to re-examine, and then overhaul, what Professor Turner wrote on the relation of the frontier to American institutions. For his brilliant papers have been the Bible, and today still constitute the central inspiration, of an extraordinary and widely held faith. That such an investigation may lead us to question, or in particulars abandon entirely, the doctrine once taught us by a beloved man is unfortunately only too obvious. But that this autopsy is necessary is the argument of the considerations advanced above, and the theme of much that follows.

How was it then — according to the essays — that the frontier affected American institutions?[3] What really was Turner's theory in this matter — and what examples did he give to support his theory? Finally, is this part of his doctrine a reasonable and useful guide to students of American history today?

The Theory of How the "Frontier" Affected American Institutions

First of all, a careful study of Turner's thirteen essays makes it plain that in theory he recognized, as all of us must do, the European origins of New World society. To the "germ theory" school of Johns Hopkins he readily conceded this much: that the first germs of things now

American had (two or three centuries before) been European. "In the settlement of America we have to observe how European life entered the continent," he wrote in 1893. ". . . Our early history is the study of European germs developing in an American environment" (page 3).

Again, Turner was willing to make two further concessions to Old World influence. In the late nineteenth century, immigrants and institutions could still be observed, pouring into the Ohio Valley and the frontier areas farther West. Of these outsiders, some were from the East, but many were obviously coming straight from Europe. Hence resulted, as Turner himself insisted, a foreign accretion to frontier society — and a sort of rural melting-pot. In the second place, the Atlantic seaboard meanwhile had remained steadily subject to the influence and suggestions of the Old World (294–295). In the East there was an obvious "tendency to adjust to a European type" (282, 68, et passim).

Notwithstanding such concessions, of course, Turner stated and restated many times a conviction that these Old World germs were not the really significant factors in our national evolution. Even in the shaping of social institutions they were merely the roots, the remote background, the undistinguished platform from which a new departure could be taken. And here it was that the frontier entered. For in Turner's view the frontier was the most important single influence in effecting that new departure. It turned European things into American

[2] The reference is to Turner's first great exposition of 1893, called "The Significance of the Frontier in American History," and to the twelve other essays or papers in this field: the whole collected and republished under the title *The Frontier in American History* (New York, 1920; hereinafter, "Turner"). Page citations in my analysis will be to this volume. I am much indebted to the publishers for permission to quote freely.

[3] Attention in this paper will be confined to *institutional* results because, in a preliminary study, "The Frontier and Frontiersmen of Turner's Essays," *The Pennsylvania Magazine of History and Biography*, LXIV, 4 (October, 1940; hereinafter, "Pierson"), 449–478, I have already subjected both Turner's definition of what the frontier *was*, and his interpretation of how it influenced the *persons* it touched, to scrutiny and challenge.

things. The longer it operated, and the farther the frontier got from the Atlantic Coast, the more overwhelming became its influence. "Too exclusive attention has been paid by institutional students to the Germanic origins, too little to the American factors," Turner insisted.

The frontier is the line of most rapid and effective Americanization. The wilderness masters the colonist. It finds him a European in dress, industries, tools, modes of travel, and thought. . . . It strips off the garments of civilization. . . . It puts him in the log cabin . . . and runs an Indian palisade around him. . . . Little by little he transforms the wilderness, but the outcome is not the old Europe, not simply the development of Germanic germs. . . . The fact is, that here is a new product that is American. . . . Thus the advance of the frontier has meant a steady movement away from the influence of Europe, a steady growth of independence on American lines (3–4).

And the grand proposal winds up with the conclusion that the novelties in American civilization finally became so successful and powerful as to react on the seaboard and on Europe itself.

By what *means* did the frontier exert so powerful a force upon society? How did it grasp an institution, tear it apart, and remold it so effectively? In his essays Turner never formulated his interpretation very succinctly. Rather he was inclined to exploit a whole congeries of explanations, shifting the burden of proof as circumstances seemed to warrant. A fair summary of his views can perhaps be organized under two heads.

First of all, as demonstrated in my analysis of his "frontier" and "frontiersmen," Turner thought of the frontier as a physical, even a savage, environment.[4]

[4] See Turner, 4, 210, *et passim;* also Pierson, 454–459 and 465–467.

At the frontier this environment was "at first too strong" for the institution, even as for the man. In a word, the wilderness "mastered" the European germs by forcing the pioneer to abandon civilized ways entirely and start completely over. "American social development has been continually beginning over again on the frontier" (2). On the other hand, whenever total elimination was not achieved, the frontier changed old ways by modifying them: that is, by forcing at least some adjustments to new physical conditions. Again, as previously stated, a new product was sometimes created through the amalgamation of populations coming from diverse countries, by a sort of rural melting-pot process (22–23). In the fourth place, the constant repetition of exposure to the new-world environment had a cumulative effect. Finally, it seems that sheer movement and migration, particularly the repetition of the pioneer business of picking up and moving on, resulted in the loss of cultural baggage on the road.

By way of a first, parenthetical criticism, it may be pointed out that this last explanation goes rather far afield. At least, it illustrates the shifting character of Turner's concept of the frontier, and raises the serious question whether the woods and migration belong in the same definition, or can have engendered identical results. If so, how are we to regard internal population movements (such as that from farm to city) that had nothing to do with the frontier? Again, what of the other great colonial migrations, to Canada, South America, and the East? Did the vast population drifts of the Mediterranean regions, or the expansion of the Norse to Iceland and the coasts of Europe, have effects comparable to those claimed for the American frontier? And are we to describe the tremendous migration of the Chinese to Manchuria in recent years in language out of Turner's essays?[5]

Clearly we have here the problem of how travel or movement affects group discipline and culture. What scholars need is less emphasis on the concept "frontier" and a deeper comparative study of migrations around the earth. Meanwhile, it may fairly be suggested that not all migrations that we have known, even in our own history, have had similar cultural effects. If movement into the Ohio Valley was disintegrating, the journey of the Pilgrims and the march of the Mormons must have been disciplinary, integrating experiences of the severest sort. But let us return to our exposition.

Thus far, Turner may be said to have been thinking of the frontier primarily in terms of nature, of geography, of physical environment. Accordingly his hypothesis postulates a kind of geographic or environmental determinism. He had not fully developed this interpretation, however, before he intruded into his definition of "frontier" — and so into his whole hypothesis — certain moral or social meanings. As I have demonstrated elsewhere, the frontier was not merely *place* and *population*, that is to say a savage wilderness and a sparse society of trappers, herders, and pioneers. It was also *process*, or more specifically the processes of conquering the continent, of moving westward, of changing from Europeans into Americans. Whether such irregularity in definition can any longer be tolerated in our use of the hypothesis is a question which has been raised before[6] and will be recurred to.

At this point, let it suffice to note that, in contrast to the geographic or natural explanations already listed, this wider concept of "frontier" introduced social and psychological reasons to account for the transformation of our institutions. Principally, the settling business affected European germs by first affecting the germ-carriers. First the wilderness process altered the character and attitudes of the men, then the men inevitably changed their institutions.

Thus, the differentiation and the Americanization of our society took place because European men, in the course of westward migration, took on the qualities that Turner chose to regard as distinctively American. Perhaps a brief recapitulation of "Americanisms" may clarify this point. Engulfed in the onward rushing torrent, fur traders, herders, and pioneers, Middle- and Far-Westerners, changed: *i.e.*, they became individualistic, optimistic, and democratic, courageous and aggressive, energetic and ambitious, rough and ready and careless of niceties, nervous and restless and adventurous, volatile and changeful, practical and materialistic; best of all, idealistic.[7]. Obviously, so great a human transformation could not but have a profound influence on the societal organism. The frontier force was operating indirectly, perhaps, but none the less powerfully. From geographic determinism, therefore, the argument had passed, by deceptively easy stages, over to a determinism of a decidedly different sort. Whether or not he fully realized the fact, Turner tended increasingly to rely for his explanations on propositions based on a sort of social psychology.

Of the two major means or forces thus postulated, now one could be detected

---

[5] I am indebted to Professor K. Asakawa of Yale University, and to Professor Owen Lattimore of the Johns Hopkins University, for stimulating comment on this point.

[6] Pierson, 462–465.

[7] Pierson, 468–476.

in obvious operation on the body of inherited institutions, now another. More
often the frontier as place and the frontier as social process were entangled and
intertwined. Whether alone or together,
however, these two forces had in theory
certain clear-cut and ascertainable effects.
They produced novelty or Americanism
in our institutions along general and
common lines. Let us ourselves pass,
therefore, from cause and from means to
an analysis of frontier results.

First of all, the essays put overwhelming theoretical emphasis on what might
be called the *idealistic improvement* that
the frontier introduced into our institutions. In part, as already hinted, improvement came from deliberate elimination of what was old, oppressive, and
unwanted. The American wilderness enabled European peoples to leave behind
aristocracies, privileges, monopolies, and
vested interests of all kinds. Hence, automatically, an increase in equality and
individual opportunity. In fact, so much
that was frozen and institutional was
intentionally abandoned that society
tended to become "atomic," and individual man once more could match his
stature against the strength of his institutions — the persistent enslaving systems
— that he or his fathers had organized.[8]

Idealistic improvement came also from
the simplification or reduction of many
of these institutions which were not
deliberately left behind. Others were
pruned or modified. Finally, by sheer
invention of devices calculated to pro-
mote a happier society, the new men of
the New World moved forward toward
the creation of a new and better civilization (better, in the author's opinion, because more free). Turner was apparently

so confident that the results of our frontier experience were liberating, and on
the whole beneficent, that the very language of his essays in dealing with this
subject took on a warm and almost lyric
quality. He urged American historians
to study "this advance"; he sang the epic
of the "imperial domain"; he returned
again and again to the confident theory
that idealism and innovation and democracy and opportunity flourished on the
frontier as nowhere else in the United
States. "From the time the mountains
rose between the pioneer and the seaboard, a new order of Americanism
arose" (18).[9]

So much for the main line of development, the line of improvement. The
reader comes now to the fact that under
the pressure of the frontier there had also
to be some loss. Turner himself admitted
that one of the effects of our experience
with so vast and rich a continent was to
make men a little careless and wasteful,
a little materialistic and anti-intellectual.
At the same time the raw and savage
wilderness could not but be unfriendly
to the delicacies and refinements of civilization, to certain higher arts, and to the
skills of the more populous and cultivated regions. Hence a kind of un-
planned loss. If not positively hostile to
morality and the social decencies, the
Westerner was often indifferent to much
that would have enriched his life and
his new society. And if not indifferent,
then he was all too frequently helpless.

Yet the essays hardly overemphasize
such defects. They are admitted as a
modest balance in a thesis that on the
whole attributes an extraordinary amount
of influence, and an extraordinary num-

---

[8] The echo of Rousseau is too strong here to be
overlooked. Note also the old American theme
of a corrupt and tyrannical Europe.

[9] For contrast, see Dixon Ryan Fox's statement
that for long years the student of civilization "as
he went west, found himself going down stairs.
. . ." "Refuse Ideas and Their Disposal," in *Ideas
in Motion* (New York, 1935), 125.

ber of beneficial results, to a partly geographic, partly sociological, frontier.

So much for pure theory. If, in the interest of a fair summary, we now postpone detailed criticism, and pass directly to a restatement of Turner's supporting evidence, one observation may nevertheless be intruded. Apparently the optimism, the buoyant localism, and the anti-European nationalism are as strong in Turner's institutional genetics as in his treatment of Western character.[10] Whether such preferences can any longer be justified in sociological theory, or maintained by historical evidence, is of course another question.

The Practical Results for Social Institutions

Let us examine next the specific proofs or illustrations advanced by Turner in the demonstration of his hypothesis. What examples did he give in his essays; what signs of frontier influence on American institutions are we advised to see?

Taking the effects in inverse order of importance, and gathering the scattered proofs together so as to bring them to bear at the appropriate points, we have first of all a series of statements indicating loss: a necessary or deliberate *abandonment*. Specifically, the material and psychological forces of the frontier are stated as having eliminated from our social inheritance the highest arts and skills. In these essays, it should be noted, Turner tended to repeat his examples, instead of elaborating or adding to them. So we find repeated statements that fine arts, literature, science, social niceties, and even the higher skills in government were necessarily sacrificed.[11] "Art, litera-

ture, refinement, scientific administration, all had to give way to this Titanic labor," he wrote in 1896 in his essay on "The Problem of the West" (211). Again, in 1901, in applying his hypothesis to the Middle West, it seemed to him that "if the task of reducing the Province of the Lake and Prairie Plains to the uses of civilization should for a time overweigh art and literature, and even high political and social ideals, it would not be surprising" (156). Again in 1910, Turner found himself urging the state university to call forth the individualism of the pioneer for finer uses: the state university "must honor the poet and painter, the writer and the teacher, the scientist and the inventor, the musician and the prophet of righteousness — the men of genius in all fields who make life nobler" (288).[12] In particular, it sometimes seemed to him that frontier democracy had "destroyed the ideals of statesmanship" (216). It refused to recognize the value or need of specialization, training, or experience in the business of government (357). It substituted rotation in office and the spoils system. It even destroyed or disregarded the codes of social and business morality (32).

Needless to say, consequences of this sort rather disturbed the champion of the frontier. Yet, as several of the foregoing extracts indicate, he was able to regard the losses as forced more by cir-

---

10 Pierson, 464–465 and 476–478.

11 Had Turner devoted much thought to the arts, in relation to the environment, he would perhaps have given more attention to architecture.

12 That is to say, the pioneering state university should honor precisely those skills and those specialists the real pioneers cared least about.

The optimistic but unfortunate employment of a word in two different senses is by no means unusual in these essays. No doubt most such errors were as unintentional and unconscious as the case here underlined. Yet they reveal Professor Turner in rather cloudy thinking; and the worst of it is that for us such lapses in precision, such vagaries of definition, subtly and slowly convert what at first seemed a brilliant illumination into a golden but impenetrable mist.

cumstance than by character, and as a temporary evil in any case. When the forest was felled, and soil and freedom were won, then the refinements of life would once again be possible. Turner's essays rank him clearly among those who defend the "cultural" shortcomings of the American people on the ground of want of time. The finer arts had simply been postponed. "As we turn from the task of the first rough conquest of the continent, there lies before us a whole wealth of unexploited resources in the realm of the spirit," was his optimistic way of recognizing the problem (309).[13] Such confidence is soothing and encouraging. Yet one may be forgiven for noticing the gulf that at this point opened before Turner's feet. If his essays mean what they appear to mean, then the doctrine is that we were most American just when we were least cultivated.[14]

To put the case a little more generously, it may perhaps be arguable that it was the novelties — not the (temporary) losses — that spelled Americanism. Yet if so, how were these innovators to remain "American," and still by and by begin to import the special skills and higher arts from Europe? Turner did not say. Rather, one suspects, the answer

is to be found in the fact that the refinements, present or absent, constituted for him a very small proportion of what was fundamentally important. His definition of "culture" was perhaps not unlike what we often think of as the typical nineteenth century American definition. A cultivated, progressive society had four parts and only four: government, business, education, and religion.[15] And the essence of these was freedom.

In the second place, according to the essays, under the pressure of the frontier our ancestral institutions and ways showed signs of *partial disintegration* and simplification. Such effects were especially noticeable in religion, finance, the law, agriculture, and group discipline.

In the field of religion, the frontier encouraged the explosion of the Protestant Church into sects and hampered religious organization. It led the pioneers out beyond the reach of all but the most indefatigable Eastern missionary. At the same time it made what worship there was a more emotional and less intellectual performance (36, 112, 165). In the field of business and finance, the pioneer developed a debtor-class psychology, a grudge against banks, and a relaxed notion of business integrity. Paper-money agitation and wild-cat banking were strong in the interior and agricultural regions (32, 210, 249). As for the law and the courts, Turner "refrained from dwelling on the lawless characteristics of the frontier, because they are sufficiently well known." He did mention the squatter, also (once each) the gambler and the desperado, the rustler and the lumber thief, and on one occasion he even called them "types of that line of scum that the waves of advancing civilization bore before them" (32–33, 272–

---

[13] Are the arts more encouraged by a rich than by a poor natural environment? May not hardship drive certain peoples to the solace of religion and the cult of beauty? Conversely, may not the materialism which sometimes results from economic success smother the artistic elements in a society? I cannot pretend to know. But sometimes it looks as if it were the drive, the will of a given population, that really mattered. Not all the hardships or poverty of history have apparently been able to squeeze out of the Jews their artistic cravings. Vice versa, Americans have sometimes given the impression of indifference, of lack of interest, rather than of any want of opportunity or time.

[14] Notice the contradiction with Turner's optimism, and the agreement with the position of Dixon Ryan Fox, cited above.

[15] I hope to be able to develop the implications of this parallel in another place.

273). Generally, however, it seemed to him sufficient to stress the frontiersman's impatience of restraints, his notion of the personality of the law, and particularly "the growth of spontaneous organs of authority" in the shape of regulators and vigilantes "where legal authority was absent" (33, 212, 254, *et passim*). Squatter sovereignty, noted Turner, was a "favorite Western political idea" (140). Finally, in the social and economic organization of the people there was a very obvious decentralization and simplification. Civilization became atomic. "Complex society is precipitated by the wilderness into a kind of primitive organization based on the family. The tendency is anti-social" (30). The tendency was also toward ethical crudity, toward ruthlessness. "The backwoodsman was intolerant of men who split hairs, or scrupled over the method of reaching the right" (254).

Thus far our analysis has relisted the destructive and regrettable results of the long and repeated exposure to primitive conditions. It is now in order to remind ourselves that Turner in his essays treated such tendencies as incidental, as unfortunate by-products of a much larger and sounder process. For the frontier could be *creative and transforming*, as well as hostile to social institutions. By what we today might call selection and cross-breeding, by psychological suggestion, even by direct material command, important *changes* were wrought in our institutions.

In the field of education, for example, despite initial handicaps, great novelties were achieved. The state universities of the Middle West, Turner thought, had been "shaped under pioneer ideals," and from them had come "the fuller recognition of scientific studies, and especially those of applied science devoted to the conquest of nature; the breaking down

of the traditional required curriculum; the union of vocational and college work in the same institution; the development of agricultural and engineering colleges and business courses. . . ." (283).[16] In a later passage, Turner likewise credited the democratic state universities with becoming "coeducational at an early date" (354).

More extensive and notable were the influences exercised by the frontier on our economy, and through our economy on our whole way of life. The continent determined the successive economic occupations. And as the hunter gave way to the herder, the cattleman to the pioneer, the unskilled pioneer to the intensive farmer, this farmer finally to the manufacturer, "the evolution of each into a higher stage has worked political transformations" (11–12). As Indian trails grew into turnpikes and railroads, so the Indian villages — likewise located by nature — gave way to trading posts, and these to cities (14). The land systems of the first Piedmont frontier — or "Old West" — set the precedents for the trans-Allegheny West, and so led to the national land policy, the preëmption acts,

16 The point cannot be argued at length here, but the reader will surely wish to look again at the essay "Pioneer Ideals and the State University." How little of what is new even our state universities owe to the environment of the frontier or the West, and how much to the inspiration of England, Germany, Switzerland, and France, one would never guess from these pages. "Other universities do the same thing," Turner admitted; "but the head springs and the main current of this great stream of tendency come from the land of the pioneers, the democratic states of the Middle West."

In 1918 the author modified his position to the extent of conceding that "the State Universities were for the most part the result of agitation and proposals of men of New England origin; but they became characteristic products of Middle Western society" (354)! In 1920, nevertheless, the assertions of the earlier essay were reprinted without qualification.

and finally, the Homestead Act (122, 170). The same back-country area in the Colonial Period "began the movement of internal trade," developed markets, and so started the slow diminution of the dependence of the Colonies on England, just as later the salt springs of the Ohio Valley freed the pioneers from dependence on the coast (108, 18, 24). The frontier, particularly as it moved away from the coast, first forced the Eastern states to fear for their population, next drew the seaports into a rivalry for its trade, and finally lured the city men from the sea into attempts to master the interior (24, 190). The crossing of the mountains put fire into Eastern veins. The problems and opportunities of the Ohio Valley proved "a tonic to this stock" (166). The "imperial resources of the great interior" engaged "the most vital activities of the whole nation" (179, 178). At last the Great Plains handed the individualist farmer his first defeat; and the Mississippi Valley became "the inciting factor in the industrial life of the nation" (147, 194). Meanwhile, the competition of the cheap lands and the drainage of the labor supply "meant an upward lift to the Eastern wage earner"; and if the mining and industrial opportunities produced a division between employer and employed, the frontier provided a safety-valve. As Turner put this matter, "the sanative influences of the free spaces of the West were destined to ameliorate labor's condition, to afford new hopes and new faith to pioneer democracy, and to postpone the problem" (193, 275, 303). Again, it was from the Piedmont and interior areas that the opposition to slavery always came (122, 173). Finally, in distinct disagreement with the North *versus* South school of interpretation of the ante-bellum period, Turner insisted that "the legislation which most devel-

oped the power of the national government, and played the largest part in its activity, was conditioned on the frontier" (24).

At this point, certain fundamental objections can no longer be postponed. In the first place, whatever may be decided as to the Piedmont (hence frontier?) origins of our land survey and sale policies, of our preëmption acts and Homestead Act, a crucial problem remains. If, as the hypothesis suggests, those first policies set precedents, if also "the squatters of Pennsylvania and the Carolinas found it easy to repeat the operation on another frontier" (122–123), what happens to the principle of originality? Here, on a small scale, we stumble into a persistent difficulty. The frontier offered novel problems, hence novelty. On the other hand, the influence of the frontier was strengthened because the exposure to it was repeated: hence copying — especially as copying was so "easy." In this instance, ought not the sale of land in rigid squares and sections (a most awkward device in rough country) to have yielded to some new and happier invention? And this, in turn, perhaps to a third, as the frontier moved westward? The implications of such questions are rather arresting.

A second far-reaching doubt arises over Turner's "imperial resources." For here, once again, we have the "frontier" being stretched to cover the whole West, and this West being defined in terms of resources. If salt, and coal, and oil, and the wealth of the continent were really the causes of institutional change, ought we not to separate them out from the frontier concept?[17]

---

[17] Note also how nature "incites" man, how inert minerals are made to draw a whole society into new forms of economy. Professor Labaree remarks on the failure of cotton fields to produce

Most dubious of all, perhaps, is the statement about the sanative and ameliorating influences of the free spaces. Granted that the exact influence and duration of the frontier as safety-valve are still under dispute, nevertheless, one conclusion seems to me inescapable. What really mattered was whether the frontier and its free land *seemed* to offer an escape, a chance to start over again. We could have had — and probably did have — land to burn, and it would have done us no good if the average man no longer saw any attraction in it. When cars, movies, and radios become essentials of the accepted standard of living, subsistence farming is repugnant even to the starving. Measured, therefore, against this concept of a changing fashion or standard of living, it may be suggested that the lure of the land began in Tudor England, before there was any available, and ceased in the United States before the available supply gave out.[18]

cotton mills, at least in the older South. But perhaps this region "incited" Manchester and Liverpool instead?

Again, according to Turnerian logic, Wilberforce and the English anti-slavery movement ought to derive from the frontier — whereas in fact the free lands of the deep South and the Southwest seem to have prolonged the career of the peculiar institution, and to have made its asperities somewhat harsher. See the reference to this point in Pierson, 471.

The ancestry and naiveté of geographical determinism have been remarked by many scholars. For an excellent résumé by Louis Wirth, see *Critiques of Research in the Social Sciences*, III (New York, 1940), 179–184.

18 For confirmation of this point of view, see the illuminating remarks of Isaiah Bowman in *The Pioneer Fringe* (American Geographical Society Special Publication No. 13, 1931), 5, 41, 74, 81, *et passim*.

In his most suggestive book *The Golden Day* (New York, 1926), page 55, Lewis Mumford has stated this point as follows: "In America the return to Nature set in before there was any physical necessity for filling up the raw lands of the West. The movement across the Alleghenies began long before the East was fully occupied:

Returning to our exposition, it is now in order to recall the tremendous emphasis and enthusiasm that Turner's hypothesis puts into the *political aspects* of frontier influence. For if our experience with the wilderness forced alterations in religion and education, in laws and in economy, it positively transformed our public administration, policies, and theory of government.

To begin, the frontier (mainly as a compelling geography) is regarded as having created and fostered sectionalism. In the Colonial Period this frontier-as-geography divided New England from Virginia, and the Middle Region from both. Later it accentuated the disharmony between North and South and set the East off from the new West. Even within the West there came to be regions whose special interests were soon reflected in industry and politics. "Indeed, the United States is, in size and natural resources, an empire, a collection of potential nations, rather than a single nation," Turner wrote. As a result its federalism would "be found to lie in the relation of sections and nation, rather than in the relation of States and nation" (158–159, 20, 52, 115, 120, 321).[19]

. . . by the time the nineteenth century was under way, the conquest of the Continent had become the obsession of every progressive community."

The difference between the frontier, as actual opportunity, and this romantic European agrarianism needs clear definition.

19 Could the influence of the frontier be uniform and centralizing, yet at the same time lead to sectionalism? Perhaps, in the sense that all frontiers, however much they differed among themselves, might have certain limited characteristics in common. To get an *increased* nationalism and an *increased* sectionalism out of the same forest is clearly a little more difficult.

It may be argued that this part of the hypothesis should be corrected by a reading of what Turner later published on "Sections." Yet Turner himself failed to repudiate his earlier statements; and what such a repudiation would have done to the "nationalizing" influence of the frontier may be gathered from the exposition that follows.

In not dissimilar fashion, the size and resources of the frontier West had a striking influence on foreign and domestic politics. The acquisition of Louisiana, for example, was "decisive" in setting the United States "on an independent career as a world power, free from entangling alliances." Again, the same expansion, by overcoming Jefferson's strict constructionism and by "swamping the New England section and its Federalism," revolutionized our political system (189, 25).

Most important of all by far, of course, the frontier made us national and made us democratic. The nationalizing influence of the frontier could hardly, it seemed to Turner, be exaggerated. It enforced unity and encouraged patriotism in many obvious and tangible ways. The menace of the Indians and the French made the frontier a consolidating agent, suggested the Albany Congress of 1754, and led to the building of forts and the creation of a national army (15–16). Again, the frontier was geographically more unified than the seaboard. Thus, toward the end of the Colonial Period, the Piedmont frontier "stretched along the western border like a cord of union" (15); while later the Mississippi Valley transfixed the barrier set up by the slavery dispute. In the third place, the mobility of population and the ease of interior communication prevented the development of provincialism (29). In the fourth place, the empty frontier regions became the melting-pot of European stocks, and even the New Englander tended to lose "the acuteness of his sectionalism" on the way through New York and Pennsylvania to the West (23, 27–28). Again, "the economic and social characteristics of the frontier worked against sectionalism"; the Middle-Western frontier developed special needs; hostility to class and regional privilege fostered a co-operative point of view;

and the abuses of the railroads and Eastern monopolies led to appeals for protection to the national government. Inevitably the frontier regions were soon trying to realize their interests in legislation. "Loose construction advanced as the nation marched westward" (25, 170–171, 189–190).

By this last, Turner meant to suggest that the frontier was responsible for much nationalistic legislation by the Federal Government, particularly in the economic field. Furthermore, such enactments automatically increased the strength of the Union and its government for general purposes thereafter. To quote Turner's proposition again, "the legislation which most developed the powers of the national government, and played the largest part in its activity, was conditioned on the frontier." "The pioneer needed the goods of the coast, and so the grand series of internal improvement and railroad legislation began, with potent nationalizing effects." "The public domain has been a force of profound importance in the nationalization and development of the government." "Administratively the frontier called out some of the highest and most vitalizing activities of the general government" (24–25). Such repetition of thought, within a very few pages, can be duplicated elsewhere in the essays (*e.g.*, 168–173) and gives a fair idea of the emphasis and conviction with which Turner kept returning to this favorite idea of his about the nationalizing influence of the frontier. Yet this last example or proof of frontier influence presents such curious internal inconsistencies that the commentator cannot forbear to pause a moment.

What Turner was thinking of, and cited again and again, was the tariff, banking, and internal improvement legislation of the period of Henry Clay on the one hand — and on the other, the Western protest movements, with their proposals for the control and reform of big business by national legislation, in the era after the Civil War.

As to the first, it is well known that Clay found supporters for his "American system" in the Ohio Valley, but is it necessary to infer that genuine frontiersmen supported the idea of the tariff or were in favor of the National Bank? The pioneers may have voted for Clay on other grounds, and in any case they appear to have voted at least as heavily for Andrew Jackson, whose opinions on the tariff were nebulous and whose views on the bank were almost unprintable. A similar fate overtakes the case for internal improvements, that is, for the theory that the frontier led the central government into the building of roads and canals. What Jackson did to the Maysville Bill is familiar to us all. And what had happened to J. Q. Adams's really national program is surely no secret. As a matter of fact, in another connection, but without realizing that he was destroying his own argument, Turner stated the case exactly. He quoted Adams as confessing, "My own system of administration, which was to make the national domain the inexhaustible fund for progressive and unceasing internal improvement, has failed." Then Turner gave the reason. "The reason is obvious; a system of administration was not what the West demanded; it wanted land" (26). That is to say, the West wanted land far more than it wanted the federal government to go into any grand series of internal improvements. How had Turner been led into his error? The answer seems to be: he had equated the West and the continent with "frontier"; and the more densely settled this area

became, the more it, as frontier, would demand internal improvements. The futility of this equation for any purposes of exact thinking is perhaps beginning to be clear.

As for the Granger and Populist and Progressive crusades, which were in part pioneer Western and which did have nationalistic implications, the difficulty is this: what had happened to the ineradicably self-reliant, *laissez-faire* individualism of the Kansas frontiersmen to make them throw up their hands? And whence came the inspiration and the very shape of the reforms they advocated?

It would seem that Turner's evidence in the matter of internal improvements, and the nationalizing effect of the frontier on economic legislation, needs further study.

But that "the most important effect of the frontier has been in the promotion of democracy here and in Europe," Turner was positive. He said so in his first great essay (30) and he stuck to the point right through to the end. The argument ran approximately as follows: the forest, the dangers, the lonely helplessness of life in the American wilderness, made the frontiersman individualistic and self-reliant. At the same time, the deliberate abandonment of European societies and the separation from the more densely settled communities of the seaboard, together with the difficulties of the journey and the confusion of races and types in the new settlements,[20] tended to destroy old social disciplines, old class arrangements, old privileges and superiorities. Finally, and most important of all, the extraordinary wealth of the continent, particularly the oppor-

[20] Note again the incorporation of non-frontier factors within the symbol "frontier."

tunity represented by the free land, gave everyone a chance to become as wealthy and self-respecting as his neighbor. Hence, the creation of a race of optimists and democrats. From democrats and from the frontier surroundings, of course, came democratic institutions.

To review Turner's presentation of this argument would require many pages,[21] but a few quotations may be useful in establishing the poetic and dogmatic flavor of his pronouncements as stated in these famous essays. "The frontier is productive of individualism," he announced (30). "The frontier individualism has from the beginning promoted democracy" (30). "Liberty and equality flourished in the frontier periods of the Middle West as perhaps never before in history" (153–154). "The Mississippi Valley has been the especial home of democracy" (190, 183). More particularly "American democracy came from the forest" (154). In translation, the word "forest" could mean many things, but generally the ingredients seem to be one part hardship, three parts free land. "Most important of all has been the fact that an area of free land has continually lain on the western border" (259). These free lands were the "gate of escape." They "promoted individualism, economic equality, freedom to rise, democracy." "In a word, then, free lands meant free opportunities. Their existence has differentiated the American democracy from the democracies which have preceded it" (259–260). Finally, in 1914, twenty-one years after his first optimistic rebellion

against the germ theory of American development, Turner put his thoughts into their most challenging and controversial form (293):

American democracy was born of no theorist's dream; it was not carried in the *Sarah Constant* to Virginia, nor in the *Mayflower* to Plymouth. It came out of the American forest, and it gained new strength each time it touched a new frontier. Not the constitution, but free land and an abundance of natural resources open to a fit people, made the democratic type of society in America for three centuries while it occupied its empire.

If this was so, what democratic institutions in particular did the American forest produce? Apparently most of those that had gained repute since 1775. First, of course, came the reforms of the Revolution and the Jeffersonian period: the abolition of entail and primogeniture, the disestablishment of the churches, the demands for public education and the abolition of slavery. "Jefferson was the first prophet of American democracy, and when we analyse the essential features of his gospel, it is clear that the Western influence was the dominant element" (250, 114).[22] From the Mississippi Valley in the thirties came manhood suffrage and all the reforms of Jacksonian democracy, including that for the elimination of imprisonment for debt (192). In the forties and fifties came new state constitutions with provisions for an elective judiciary. Finally, after the Civil War, the Mississippi Valley and the Plains gave birth to the Granger and Greenback movements, and to the

---

[21] For example, it is not always clear what Turner meant by the word "democrats"; it is, as Beard warns, by no means certain that there ever was much "individualism" on the frontier; and one would hardly guess from Turner's pages how inharmonious free opportunity and equalitarianism sometimes are (Pierson, 468–472).

[22] The student will note that T. P. Abernethy is also skeptical of the frontier explanation of Thomas Jefferson. See especially his Author's Preface to *Three Virginia Frontiers* (University of Louisiana, 1940), x.

Populist crusade. Bryan Democracy and the Republicanism of Theodore Roosevelt "were Mississippi Valley ideals in action" (203–204).

The reader will recall that Benjamin F. Wright and a number of others have long since perceived and stated the surprising poverty of at least certain frontier areas in democracy and in political invention. Yet a few additional queries may legitimately be raised at this point. For instance, are we really prepared to ascribe the platform of the Populists and the reforms of Progressivism to the frontier? Does not the history of social legislation in England and on the Continent indicate a quite different explanation? Again, it would appear that the woman suffrage idea originated in Europe and found but slim support in the Ohio Valley. The direct dependence of our belated Civil Service legislation on the earlier English movement will be apparent to anyone who cares to investigate that subject. As for manhood suffrage, whatever may have been the contributions of the wilderness frontier, is it not hard to believe that the American democrat sprang, as it were, full-armed, ballot in hand, out of the Western woods? Surely one cannot today dismiss the long evolution of Parliament, the history of Colonial legislatures, the methods of the New England town meeting, the self-government of Congregational churches, and the voting habits of trading-company stockholders without a thought. This leads to another disconcerting observation. Turner nowhere seriously credits Anglo-American Protestantism (what Tocqueville so discerningly called our "republican religion") with democratic tendencies. One is left to infer that such equalitarian and humanitarian interests as American Christianity has displayed must have derived from the experience of conquering the West.

Thus, to conclude our exposition of the Turner hypothesis, the West's "steady influence toward democracy" was not without its influence on the East, and on Europe. It was not until the early nineteenth century, and then "largely by reason of the drainage of population to the West, and the stir in the air raised by the Western winds of Jacksonian democracy, that most of the older States reconstructed their constitutions on a more democratic basis. From the Mississippi Valley . . . came the inspiration for this era of change" (192). The possibility that their citizens might escape to practically free land "compelled the coastwise States to liberalize the franchise; and it prevented the formation of a dominant class, whether based on property or on custom" (274, 30, 172, 185). As for Europe, what it derived from the frontier is less clear. The frontier is asserted to have turned both pioneer and Easterner away from Europe, and to have been the goal of peasant and artisan, the mecca for Europe's idealists and social reformers, through three hundred years (261–262, 349).[23]

"The men of the Mississippi Valley compelled the men of the East to think in American terms instead of European." When cities and sections turned their energies to the interior, "a genuine American culture began" (185, 190).

General Criticism

Turner's theoretical system, with proof and illustration, has now been developed and quoted at sufficient length to en-

[23] That numerous idealists and reformers were drawn out of old Europe into the new West is certain, but it may be that the empty woods were more hospitable (*i.e.*, less hostile) to Utopian experiments than were frontier populations.

able us to proceed to the next step: an attempt at an overall criticism.

First, then, let me say emphatically that it would seem small-minded to forget or to depreciate the inspiration that these essays originally offered to historians. Nor does it seem that we, of half a century later, have yet heard arguments that would warrant us in discarding the celebrated hypothesis entirely, out of hand. Too much of Turner's interpretation still seems reasonable, and corresponding to fact. Even in so condensed an analysis as has just been offered, the poetic insights and the masterful grasp of an understanding mind are hardly to be disguised. No blanket repudiation is therefore here to be proposed.

On the other hand, Turner himself did make a number of flat-footed and dogmatic statements, did put forward some highly questionable interpretations, did on occasion guess and not verify, did exaggerate — and stick for more than twenty years to the exaggerations. Hence it would seem that, however badly the master may have been served by his students and continuers in other particulars, these followers have been made the scapegoats a little too hastily. For they have not alone been responsible for the palpable errors and exaggerations that many of the rising generation recognize in the frontier theory as it is stated and applied today. At least they did not invent the safety-valve theory that now looks so dubious; they didn't misquote when they attributed political invention, and most of the reforms and the reformers, to the frontier;[24] they weren't the first local and national patriots. In his work with his students, Turner seems to have been modest and tentative and open-minded to a degree; but in his essays he could be and was as inclusive and sweeping as any have been since.

What were the statements and attitudes which we regard as extreme or with which we would disagree? A number have just been alluded to, or were earlier marked and commented upon. But the treatment has been parenthetical and fragmentary. Let me conclude, therefore, with a brief organization of the most cogent reasons for regarding Turner's original doctrine on the frontier and American institutions as defective and in need of repair.

To begin with the details and proceed to the general, it seems first of all necessary to suggest that — whatever may later be decided about Turner's theory — his evidence and proofs leave much to be desired. I am not here referring to our difficulty in accepting Turner's reasons for believing that the frontier stimulated invention, liberal ideas, educational improvements, or humanitarian reforms — a difficulty that remains substantial enough in itself. Rather, it is the quantity of his evidence to which I would now call attention. How few were his concrete examples, and how often he would repeat them is really astonishing. For twenty-seven years he kept the same happy illustrations, in the same language often, and even perhaps without testing them by fresh investigation. In his first essay Turner invited such testing, and suggested the specific investigation of a number of different frontiers: "It would be a work worth the historian's labors to mark these various frontiers and in de-

---

[24] In an 1899 version of his first great essay, Turner did grant that "the study of the evolution of western institutions shows how slight was the proportion of actual theoretical invention of institutions." But for some reason this reservation was thereafter omitted from his thesis. See *The Early Writings of Frederick Jackson Turner* (Madison, Wisconsin, 1938), 38.

tail compare one with another" (10). Yet if one goes to the later frontier essays for demonstration, one finds it only in the most general and vague terms. Undoubtedly, Turner was more interested in discovering than in proving. Undoubtedly, also, he must on occasion have carried his analysis of special areas and his search for positive proof somewhat deeper, particularly in his work with his graduate students and in his study of the different sections. Unfortunately, there is astonishingly little to show for that research in the later essays.

Did Turner, perhaps, on the other hand, put his effort into theory and philosophy, into developing and revising his first grand vision and interpretation? Once again, curiously, our examination indicates that he did not. For not only did he republish his first essay without substantial alteration, but his later essays show little if any advance beyond the position taken in his first. Not only is there small proof of fresh research; there is as little proof of fresh thinking.[25] Elaboration, progress in application, repetition, certainly, but distressingly little in the way of genuine reconsideration or modification. If anything, the later essays are more general, sweeping, and blurred — as if the hypothesis had somewhere already been proved. Yet when one turns back to the first statement one is startled to find in it reservations, moderation, and doubt.

A critic is reduced, therefore, to finding the same theory throughout, and is moved to protest at certain aspects of that theory. It is dangerous and ungenerous,

25 Considerable awareness of the capture of the Middle West by industrialism appears, but this leads toward discouragement or exhortation rather than to a revision in frontier theory.

I acknowledge, for a man living in a later climate of opinion to disparage the attitude of an earlier day. But since our problem concerns the *present applicability and future usefulness* of these frontier essays, certain assumptions and definitions cannot be allowed to pass without challenge.

As has been pointed out, first of all, the essays are in a high degree unsatisfactory in clarity, or definition. Turner's Master Force is defined and used as area, as population, as process. As if such inharmonious and confusing interpretations were not sufficiently inclusive, this force is then made to cover soil and mineral resources as well, — and at times everything Western, or pre-industrial, or non-European! I think it fair to say that the word "frontier" has been, and will be found again, a Pandora's box of trouble to historians, when opened to such wide interpretation.

Again, there seems to be haziness in the statement of *means,* and real doubt as to many of the *results* claimed for the frontier. At moments the wilderness, and even the flow of our population westward, seem to have been destructive rather than constructive experiences. And when the rebuilding is scrutinized, the proportion of invention looks surprisingly small. In particular, the contribution of the frontier to our educational, economic, and political institutions needs cautious reappraisal.

Once again, the emotional attitudes or assumptions of the author — and of his generation? — color his essays unmistakably. It would have been strange had they not done so. No personal censure is therefore intended. On the other hand, for the interpretation of American history in 1942, the emphasis of 1893 may become a serious handicap; it may even obscure or distort the elements in the theory that are still most meaningful. To be specific, the frontier hypothesis seems — as has been indicated several times already — too optimistic, too romantic, too provincial,[26] and too nationalistic to be reliable in any survey of world history or study in comparative civilization. And it is too narrowly sectional and materialistic — in the sense of assigning deterministic forces to physical environment — to seem any longer a satisfactory gauge for internal cause-measurements. A thoughtful reading of the thirteen essays, or even of such materials as it has been possible to quote in this paper, ought to be conclusive on these defects. Yet perhaps a word more about one or two of them will not be out of place.

At an earlier point in the argument, the migration factor was isolated — as a sort of foreign substance — out of the frontier concept; and it was suggested that, at the least, a comparison with city-ward movements and with migrations the world around is in order. It now seems pertinent to suggest the extension of such comparisons from migration to the *whole story of settlement* or environmental adjustment in South America, Australia, and Africa. Did comparable situations always produce comparable results? Moreover, if we repeat such comparisons *within* the American experience, do we really find much similarity between the frontiers of Colonial Massachusetts, the Mississippi Delta, the Plains, and the mining country? If not, it would appear that the applicability of Turner's frontier hypothesis is far more limited than has been supposed.

Along another line of thought, I have suggested that Turner's views were deterministic. They were almost fatalistic.[27] Again and again one gets the impression that western man was in the grip of overpowering forces. "The people of the United States have taken their tone from the incessant expansion which has not only been open but has even been forced upon them" (37, 4, 211).

Now what makes this determinism particularly questionable is the fact that it is materialistic, yet in a high degree confused and cloudy in its statement of causes. Turner has been attacked by the economic determinists for not regarding commercialism, industrialism, and capitalism as more important than the continent — and the frontier essays certainly pay far too little attention to the commercial character of nineteenth-century American society, East *or* West. This school of critics is also quite correct in labelling Turner a geographer and a sociologist rather than a champion of the Marxian dialectic or interpretation.[28] Nevertheless Turner remains, in his own way, almost as convinced a materialist as the author of *Das Kapital* himself. Only Turner's mastering force is a multiple thing, a cluster of causes singularly disparate and inharmonious. Part of the

[27] This is shown, in a kind of inverted fashion, by the pessimism to which the disappearance of the safety-valve frontier has given rise. I do not suppose that Turner invented this "escape" concept. The pioneering legends, from which his hypothesis must itself have derived, have doubtless exercised their own share of influence, quite independently. Yet if today our leaders still hitch our star to a covered wagon, the frontier theory may share the responsibility.

[26] The hypothesis is "provincial" in two different ways; it ignores frontiers in other lands, and it slights one whole side of human culture in the United States.

[28] This accusation would seem one to be borne quite cheerfully. To the present writer, the substitution of *economic man* for *frontier man* would constitute a most doubtful improvement.

time the essays cite the natural environment, the physical continent, the wilderness; at other moments the source of change is located in the state of society: the sparseness, mobility, or indiscipline of settlement. Admittedly, America represented both physical hardship and social opportunity. The West was rough (a geographic factor) and it was empty (a sociological force). Perhaps, then, Turner's greatest achievement was his successful marriage of these two dissimilar forces in the single phrase: *free land*. He did not invent the term or the ideas it contains. But he most certainly popularized them.

If this sounds like a defense of Turner, it is intended rather as a clearer definition of his special materialism, which remains objectionable. And it remains so — even disregarding the untenable variations in his definition of "frontier" — because too much is attributed both to the land and to the fact that it was easy to acquire. A number of Turner's ablest friends and admirers regard his "free land" doctrine as a contribution of extraordinary insight and importance, and unquestionably it does seem impressive. Yet the modern observer cannot but be disturbed by the failure of some non-English groups, and even of a tremendous number of native Americans, to heed this call. The open spaces do not seem to have acted as a solvent on the Pennsylvania Germans or the *habitants* of Lower Canada, and the migratory New England groups were only partially disintegrated, while an increasing number of farm boys gravitated to town and city (an even stronger solvent?) instead. It will bear repeating that Turner perhaps exaggerated the importance of "free land."[29]

[29] Perhaps it is unreasonable to suggest that the North American Indians ought to have profited in

On the other hand, I cannot but feel that too small a role is allowed to man's own character and ambitions, to his capacity for change, and to the traditions and momentum of the society which came to use this free land. Thus the continent masters, destroys, commands, and creates — while man is surprisingly passive. Where many of us are inclined to regard the physical environment as permissive, or limiting in its influence, Turner in his essays tends to make it mandatory. Vice versa, where sociologists are today coming to recognize the factor of tradition and habit as very powerful, and where a man's ability to master circumstance is at times conceded to be extraordinary, the frontier hypothesis tends to ignore human origins and peculiarities, at least in the composition of American traits and American institutions. Thus first causes are made to lie in real estate, not state of mind. Hence, again, the first Colonial settlers are not examined with any care, but are treated as if they were *average* Europeans. And the later developments and changes in coastal society are handled as if they could have had only two sources: either a fresh migration or influence from Europe, or the powerful influence of an innovating frontier. Native invention in New England? Improvement in New

the same fashion from so much free land. Yet what about the Spaniards, who had the run of the whole hemisphere? Did the Mississippi Valley make them democratic, prosperous, and numerous? In a word, do not the level of culture, and the "fitness" of a society for the wilderness, matter more than the wilderness? Employing again the comparative vista, were there no unoccupied forests in medieval France? And if today a new continent were to rise out of the Pacific Ocean, are we so sure that it would encourage small freeholds, not corporation or governmental monopolies? (For stimulus and clarification on this point I am indebted to the professors and students of history at the Johns Hopkins University.)

York without the stimulus of the West? Apparently not.[30]

The Contradictions and Omissions

It remains to add two final comments. They concern contradiction and omission.

However optimistic, nationalistic, one-sided, repetitious, fatalistic, undocumented, or erroneous a number of Turner's proposals may appear, the curious fact seems to be that one of the most striking weaknesses of the essays as a whole is internal inconsistency. As has been hinted throughout this paper, the frontier theory in its full development does not hang together. The nationalism of the frontier does violence to its sectional tendencies, innovations are derived from repetition, the improvement of civilization is achieved *via* the abandonment of civilization, and materialism gives birth to idealism. Such inconsistencies do not necessarily condemn the whole theory out of hand. But they do unsettle conviction; they make it hard to remain complacent; they invite the most careful, open-minded restudy.

To this should be added the thought of what Turner did not write. Making all due allowances for the fact that the master's essays were composed in the

period 1893–1920, it remains true that in the single field of economics he slighted the industrial revolution, he didn't seem to understand the commercial revolution, and he said nothing at all about the agricultural revolution. Yet it might be asserted that the last alone will be found to have produced more changes in American farming in the nineteenth century than all the frontiers put together! Again, it must be clear from our restatement that the frontier essays entirely failed to check the hypothesis by setting American experience against world experience. Because Turner was primarily a *Western* explorer, his pupils and followers have tended to neglect the all-important comparative approach. When, then, we review the questions with which this paper began, when we remember that the thirteen frontier essays treat the development of "American" and Middle-Western characteristics without reference to Romanticism, to Evangelism, to the eighteenth-century Enlightenment, to the scientific discoveries and the secularization of thought that in varying degrees have overtaken all Western peoples since the discovery of America, it may fairly be deduced that *for future purposes* these celebrated statements leave too much out.

Perhaps a conclusion may be stated in these terms:

In what it proposes, the frontier hypothesis needs painstaking revision. By what it fails to mention, the theory today disqualifies itself as an adequate guide to American development.

---

[30] Turner did not write thirteen essays on the frontier without recognizing that the frontier area in which New Englanders settled turned out somehow different. Again he spoke of Germans in Wisconsin, of Scandinavian immigration, and the like. But by and large, it was the land these immigrants went to rather than the traits they came with, that seemed to Turner *significant*.

Carlton J. H. Hayes: THE AMERICAN FRONTIER— FRONTIER OF WHAT?

IT is now over half a century since Frederick Jackson Turner assisted in Chicago at the international celebration of the discovery of America by reading his famous paper on "The Significance of the Frontier in American History." "Almost without critical test," as Professor Paxson has remarked, the frontier hypothesis in that paper met with prompt and well-nigh unanimous acceptance by historians of the United States.[1] And during succeeding years, we all know, it has inspired and been exploited in a multitude of tomes and monographs. Nowadays none of our university departments of history is complete without a frontier specialist, and no one, even a New Yorker, would essay a history of the United States, whether for the profession, the general reader, or the schools, without paying homage to the Turner hypothesis.

Our historical guild should have no illusion or pessimism about its ability, in the long run, to lodge in popular consciousness practically any interpretation or reconstruction of the past upon which it may concentrate. It can certainly perceive and rejoice that its concentration for a half century on the significance of the frontier in American history has been productive not only of caviar for semi-

[1] Frederic L. Paxson, in *Encyclopedia of the Social Sciences*, XV (1935), 132–33.

nars but of common fare for journalists and radio commentators. The hypothesis has become axiomatic that our democracy and social progress and national mores have been chiefly, if unconsciously, the creation of frontiersmen, as these, in an epic sweep westward across the continent, successively wrested new free lands from the wilderness and the Indians and there, "as nowhere else in recorded history, set up institutions relatively free from coercion by either law or habit."

I have neither the intention nor the competence to criticize this hypothesis. I can only bow, with respect and envy, to the numerous scholars in American history who, with extraordinary industry and enthusiasm, and in great detail, have applied and tested it during the last half century. I wonder, however, if the time has not come when our historians might profitably broaden their conception of the frontier and extend their researches and writing into a wider field. For granting that the frontier has been a major factor in the historical conditioning and development of what is distinctive in the United States, a large and now, I believe, most pertinent question remains about the American frontier. It is a frontier of what?

This would seem an obvious question, with an obvious answer. The answer was,

From the *American Historical Review*, 51 (January, 1946), 199–210, 216, by permission of the publisher.

indeed, clearly indicated several years ago by the late President Dixon Ryan Fox in a series of brilliant essays,[2] and likewise by the late Professor William R. Shepherd in his graduate lecture course and seminar on European expansion and in articles he published in the *Political Science Quarterly*.[3] Both those scholars, and a considerable number of others, including the California "school" of Professor Herbert Bolton, regarded the advancing frontier in North America, like similar frontiers in South America, Australasia, and South Africa, as a frontier of Europe. They were concerned with the transit of culture from Europe, or from already Europeanized oversea areas, to the frontier, as well as with the reverse cultural influences of the frontier.

Unfortunately, such broad vision was shared by relatively few specialists in American history, and it led to no appreciable lessening of their absorption in the frontier itself and in the one-way influences of the frontier upon purely American developments. One conventionally assumed that the frontier was a western frontier of the eastern United States. It was viewed as a peculiarly American phenomenon, determining the unique character of our own national society and culture.

2

The vogue of this restricted interpretation of the American frontier, and the concurrent neglect of broader and otherwise obvious considerations, have been, I submit, at once a result and a stimulant of growing intellectual isolationism in

[2] Most notably, his "Civilization in Transit," "Culture in Knapsacks," and "Refuse Ideas and Their Disposal," conveniently assembled in D. R. Fox, *Ideas in Motion* (New York, 1935). The first of these appeared originally in the *American Historical Review*, XXXII (1927), 753–68.

[3] *Political Science Quarterly*, XXXII (1919), 43–60, 210–25, 392–412.

the United States. Our isolationism, of course, has many aspects, political and economic as well as intellectual, and many explanations. Before the days of steamships and airplanes we were, in truth, remote from the rest of the world; and our achievement of political independence naturally fostered an ambition for intellectual independence. Moreover, a lurking suspicion of inferiority, which long lingered with us, has had the usual psychological compensation in strident assertion of superiority. And for utilitarian purposes, as well as under romantic influences, we have cultivated a lusty nationalism, the more intense because the more artificial. In Europe, everybody has been conscious of belonging to a particular nationality, with distinctive language and traditions, and nationalism has been a more or less natural flowering of the consciousness of nationality. In the United States, on the other hand, nationalism has been the fertilizer, rather than the flower. It has here been spread and utilized as the most effective means of producing in a population of very diverse origins — linguistic, religious, and racial — a common and luxuriant consciousness of belonging to a new and unique nationality. All this has inoculated us against Europe and built up an isolationist state of mind.

In all this, too, our historiography has played no inconsiderable part. It was marked, in the first generation of our political independence, by patriotic and panegyrical works, shelved now but influential then, such as David Ramsay's *History of the American Revolution*, Timothy Pitkin's *Political and Civil History of the United States of America*, and the biographies of Washington by Mason Weems and John Marshall. Afterwards, for two succeeding generations and well into the 1880's, its central monument was

George Bancroft's elaborate presentation of American history as an unfolding of the Deity's grand design to enshrine in the New World and particularly in the United States the ark of the covenant of liberty and democracy.

Since the introduction, in the 1870's and 1880's, of professional university training, with its inculcation of scientific spirit and methods, American historiography has understandably reacted against the puerilities of a "Parson" Weems and the grandiose pietism of a Bancroft. Yet, if our historical writing has latterly become more critical in manner, it is not less American in subject matter and emphasis. Indeed, a striking general fact about it during the past seventy years has been the tendency to turn away from European themes and to concentrate upon strictly American. The seventy years mark a new and self-imposed sort of "Babylonian Captivity." There have been no real successors to Prescott, Motley, and Parkman; our recent literary historians write epics of the United States.

For every monograph or doctoral dissertation in European history during the past twenty years, there have been at least a dozen in American history. And whereas formerly every research worker in American history had had some basic training in medieval or modern European history, nowadays one can, and frequently does, produce a dissertation in a state of comparative innocence about what has occurred outside the geographical confines of the United States. This circumstance and the narrowing specialized training of our university seminars must explain why so many younger investigators of the American frontier have neglected its broader relationships and been indifferent to its comparative study. Even the growing number of economic determinists among us tend more and more to seek confirmation of their faith in exclusively American events.

Yet apparently the isolationist and nationalist trend in American historiography is not deemed fast or effective enough. In the columns of a leading metropolitan newspaper is alarmingly broadcast a series of embarrassing disclosures that there are "facts" of American history which high-school and college graduates have not learned, or do not remember. To remedy the sorry situation, state laws are being rapidly enacted by politicians addicted to Fourth of July oratory, and curriculums are being correspondingly refashioned by professional "educators." We are going to compel the next generation to have more American history — and, perforce, less of any other: the very generation which we expect to carry successfully the new and manifold international responsibilities we have assumed.

Of course the backbone of the schooling of our young people should be history — solid, vertebrate history — and not any of the amorphous jelly-like substitutes for it which were a fad with curriculum-makers between the first and second World Wars. But I, for one, do not see how we substantially improve matters by expanding a high-school course in American history from one year to two or three and telescoping all the rest of man's past and the history of all other nations into a single year or half year of fleeting elementary generalization quaintly described as "world history." Nor do I perceive how a college sequence or a university doctorate in "American civilization" is going to prepare our students and scholars for enlightened participation in the transcendent responsibilities of the United States as a world power, that is, unless "American civilization" is intimately and historically related to the original and widely ramifying civilization of which it is but a fragment.

The present trend, if unchecked, can only confirm the popular myths that the "American way of life" is something entirely indigenous, something wholly new, and something vastly superior to any other nation's. It is also likely to strengthen our people's missionary and messianic impulse, which will have far greater scope and far greater opportunity for expressing itself in the current aftermath of the second World War, and which, if unattended by realistic knowledge of other peoples and their historic cultures, may lead to the most dangerous consequences for the United States itself. Just when we are recognizing the futility of political isolation and joining at long last an international security organization, and when, through reciprocal trade agreements and acceptance of the Bretton Woods proposals, we are abandoning efforts at economic isolation, it is astonishing and paradoxical that at the same time we should keep alive and actually intensify an intellectual isolationism.

From the bitter experiences of recent years, we, as a nation, have derived surprisingly few lessons affecting our thinking. We have doubtless become a bit more aware of some kind of relationship between the United States and the world outside, and more inclined to wishful thoughts about a universal utopia which our sanguine publicists alluringly, though vaguely, picture as "the bright new world of tomorrow." Doubtless, too, certain patent strategic needs of the moment, coupled with a good deal of public advertising, have aroused a special interest in Latin America and popularized the concept of "hemispheric solidarity," which probably signifies, however, only a shift of isolationism from the nation to the hemisphere. At any rate, there can be no doubt that the bulk of Americans, including the bulk of our so-called intellectuals, continue to think, in essentially isolationist terms, of separate "Old World" and "New World," of detached Eastern and Western Hemispheres, of "Europe for the Europeans" and "America for the Americans."

This dichotomy in our thinking is the result, let me repeat, of ignorance, of self-centered absorption in local or sectional concerns, and of nationalist propaganda. It is unrealistic, contrary to basic historical facts, and highly dangerous for our country at the present and in the future.

3

We used to know that we were Europeans as well as Americans, that we were not Indians or a people miraculously sprung from virgin forests like the primitive Germans described by Tacitus, but modern Europeans living in America on a frontier of Europe. All our original white ancestors on this continent knew they came from Europe. They and their sons and grandsons knew they had ties with Englishmen, Spaniards, Portuguese, Hollanders, or Frenchmen, as the case might be, not only on this side of the ocean but on the other. And generation after generation of their descendants on this side, no matter on what segment of the frontier they chanced to be, and no matter how intent on clearing new lands, were concerned and found themselves participants in all the successive major wars of Europe from the sixteenth century to the twentieth: the English-Spanish wars, the English-Dutch wars, the War of the League of Augsburg, the War of the Spanish Succession, the War of the Austrian Succession, the Seven Years' War, the Revolutionary and Napoleonic

Wars, the war of 1914, the war of 1939. From the first, moreover, it has been known or knowable, if latterly obscured, that our language, our religion, our culture are rooted in Europe, that our ideals of liberty and constitutional government are a heritage of Europe.

In paying tribute to the members of the Constitutional Convention of 1787, Charles A. Beard has remarked:

It is not merely patriotic pride that compels one to assert that never in the history of assemblies has there been a convention of men richer in political experience and in practical knowledge, or endowed with a profounder insight into the springs of human action and the intimate essence of government. It is indeed an astounding fact that at one time so many men skilled in statecraft could be found on the very frontiers of civilization among a population numbering about four million whites.[4]

It is not quite so astounding, I would add, if one bears in mind that those men "on the very frontiers of civilization" possessed lively contacts with, and solid knowledge of, the European civilization on whose frontiers they were. One has only to run through the numbers of the *Federalist* to recognize the sure and firm grasp of such men as Hamilton, Madison, and Jay on the history and political experience of ancient Greece and Rome and of the countries of medieval and modern Europe — Britain, Germany, France, Poland, the Netherlands, Switzerland.[5] The founding fathers may have been frontiersmen and greatly influenced by economic conditions in the New

World, but they could readily have passed a searching examination for the doctorate in European history and European comparative government, which, I dare say, is more than the majority of our senators or even of our Ph.D.'s in American history could now do.

That the United States could become an independent nation and enjoy the freedom and opportunity to extend its frontiers and greatly to increase its population and prosperity and strength during the perilous fifty years of Revolutionary and Napoleonic Wars and Metternichean reaction, from 1775 to 1825, is attributable less to American aloofness from Europe than to the informed statecraft of Americans who were then in familiar touch with Europe and equipped to treat with it intelligently and realistically. Almost without exception, our presidents and secretaries of state and key diplomatists of that time had practical experience in European, as well as American, affairs — Franklin, Jefferson, Jay, Marshall, Madison, Monroe, John Adams, John Quincy Adams. Monroe, for example, served in diplomatic posts in France, England, and Spain for six years before he became Madison's Secretary of State, and his own Secretary of State, John Quincy Adams, had been a student at Paris and Leiden and had had twenty years' diplomatic experience in France, the Netherlands, Prussia, Russia, and Great Britain. The words which this qualified statesman put into Monroe's celebrated message of 1823 to the Congress expressed an enlightened realism in notable contrast with utterances and actions of certain American statesmen of a later date less in touch with the realities of Europe and more with ideological propaganda in America.

Said the message of 1823, without trace of a holier-than-thou attitude:

[4] Charles A. Beard, *The Supreme Court and the Constitution* (New York, 1912), pp. 86–87.

[5] See in particular Nos. 17–20, 34, 47, and 63 of the *Federalist,* in the convenient sesquicentennial reprint, edited by Edward Mead Earle (Washington, 1939).

Our policy in regard to Europe . . . remains the same, which is, not to interfere in the internal affairs of any of its powers; to consider the Government *de facto* as the legitimate Government for us; to cultivate friendly relations with it, and to preserve those relations by a frank, firm, and manly policy; meeting, in all instances, the just claims of every power; submitting to injuries from none.

It was not only our statesmen of that time who knew and appreciated the relationship between Europe and America. Our colleges and academies, with their classical curriculum, and our literary men and publicists, with their extensive reading of British and French philosophers of the seventeenth and eighteenth centuries, possessed like knowledge and appreciation. Our commercial classes, including our cotton planters, had it, too. To protect our commerce with Europe, Jefferson dispatched to the Mediterranean an American armed expeditionary force which made landings in North Africa nearly a century and a half before the recent repetition of American campaigning in the Mediterranean. And what a reading public there was in the United States for those literary historians in our "middle period" — Irving, Prescott, Motley, and Parkman — who dwelt on exploits of Spanish, Dutch, and French. It might well be envied by any historian of the American frontier or even by the Book-of-the-Month Club. The Mediterranean Sea was not then so far off, or the Atlantic Ocean so wide, as our developing isolationist nationalism later made them.

Our successive American generations of frontiersmen on the eastern seaboard, in the Piedmont, across the Alleghenies, along the Ohio, the Great Lakes, and the Mississippi, over the prairies, and into and beyond the Rockies, may have thought of themselves as Americans first. They may have adopted Indian dress and Indian usages in hunting and fishing and scalping. They may have exerted, and doubtless did exert, a profound and lasting influence on the nationalist evolution of the United States. But all this did not make them Indians or immunize them against the superior and eventually mastering civilization which emanated from Europe and relentlessly followed them. They remained Europeans and retained at least the rudiments of European civilization. After all, the American frontier, as Professor Turner so ably and perhaps regretfully showed, was an evanescent phenomenon, ever passing from primitiveness toward the social and intellectual pattern of the area in back of it. In other words, the abiding heritage of traditional civilization outweighed, in a relatively brief period, the novelties acquired from Indians and wilderness. Continuity proved stronger than change. The transit of culture was not so much *from* as *to* the frontier.

Differences admittedly obtain between Americans in the United States and the peoples in Europe from whom they are descended, but the differences are not greater in kind, and hardly greater in degree, than those obtaining between Englishmen and Spaniards or between Germans and Italians, or between the people of the United States and the peoples of Central and South America. True, the nationalism which has progressively infected all peoples of Europe and America during the last hundred and fifty years has grossly exaggerated the differences and given wide currency to the notion of distinctive and self-contained national cultures — a French culture, a Norwegian culture, a Spanish culture, an American culture. The result has been an obscuring and neglect of what these several national cultures have in common, a European or "Western" culture, the community of heritage and outlook and interests in Europe and its whole American frontier.

Actual differences are differences of emphasis and detail, associated with political sovereignty and independence, and arising from variant geographical and historical circumstances. Back of them all, however, is a unifying fact and force, which is describable as "European" or "Western," and which, now more than ever before, needs to be appreciated and applied. Actually and fundamentally, just as the European remains a European while thinking of himself first as an Englishman, a Frenchman, a German, or a Spaniard, so the descendants of Europeans in America remain European even while insisting that they are Americans first.

The frontier has undoubtedly been a very important source of what is distinctive and peculiar in the national evolution of the United States. But few European nations have been without a frontier in the American sense at some time in their history and without significant lasting effects of that frontier. Contemporary peculiarities in the life and customs of Spain, for instance, cannot be dissociated from the slow advance, during several centuries, of a frontier of conquest of Moorish lands; nor Germany's, from an analogous frontier in barbarous regions of north central Europe. In a larger way, all America is a frontier: Latin America, of Spain and Portugal; Quebec, of France; the United States, of Great Britain and Holland, Spain and France, Germany and Ireland, Scandinavia and Italy and Poland. Our Negroes and Indians, as these have been civilized, have been Europeanized as

well as Americanized. The "melting pot" is no novelty in the history of Western civilization; it has latterly been doing in America, on a large scale, the same sort of fusing which at earlier dates produced the chief nations of modern Europe. Comparative study of frontiers in Europe and America, together with comparative study of melting pots and nationalisms in both, might serve to demonstrate that obvious differences between nations of European tradition are fewer and relatively less significant than their similarities.

4

"European," as I here use the term, does not refer merely to a detached piece of geography or to a continent by itself, and not to another "hemisphere" or a hoary and pitiable "Old World." Rather, it refers to a great historic culture, the "Western" civilization, which, taking its rise around the Mediterranean, has long since embraced the Atlantic, creating what Mr. Walter Lippmann has appropriately designated the "Atlantic Community."[6] As Professor Ross Hoffman says:

Every state of the North and South American continents originated from Western European Christendom which Voltaire, in the age before the independence movements, characterized so well as a "great republic." Englishmen, Frenchmen, Spaniards, Portuguese, Dutchmen and Danes in the early modern centuries made the Atlantic Ocean the inland sea of Western civilization; they made it an historical and geographical extension of the Mediterranean. . . . Many of these early-forged bonds still span the Atlantic, and the spread of British, French, and American ideals of liberty and constitutional government has made this oceanic region the cit-

6 Walter Lippmann, *U. S. War Aims* (Boston, 1944), pp. 63–88.

adel of what today is rather loosely called Democracy.[7]

Of such an Atlantic community and the European civilization basic to it, we Americans are co-heirs and co-developers, and probably in the future the leaders. If we are successfully to discharge our heavy and difficult postwar responsibilities, we shall not further weaken, but rather strengthen, the consciousness and bonds of this cultural community.

Against it, militate two current trends of quite contradictory character. One, which I have already indicated, is the nationalistic tendency to view each nation as *sui generis*, and to attribute to it an independent and distinctive culture all its own. The second is the hypothesizing of a "world civilization." This has already passed from the fictional titles of high-school textbooks to the solemn pronouncements of statesmen. It represents a leap from myopic nationalism to starry-eyed universalism. I, for one, have not the faintest idea what world civilization is. I know there are enduring and respectable civilizations in Moslem areas, in India, in China, and presumably in Japan. I also know there are considerable influences of such civilizations upon ours, and, especially in the material domain, heavy impacts by ours upon them. But the many existing civilizations still do not constitute a single "world civilization," and for a long time to come, I hazard, the common denominator among them is likely to be low — as low, I should suppose, as unadorned "human nature."

Neither devotion to one's nation nor idealization of the world at large should

obscure the important cultural entities which lie between. These are the power-houses of civilization for their constituent nationalities, and the units which must be brought into co-operation for any world order of the future. The one to which Americans belong is the "European" or "Western." It has conditioned our past. And whether we are aware of it, or not, it conditions our present and future.

In what does it consist? First, in the Greco-Roman tradition, with its rich heritage of literature and language, of philosophy, of architecture and art, of law and political concepts. Second, in the Judeo-Christian tradition, with its fructifying ethos and ethics, its abiding and permeating influence on personal and social behavior, its constant distinctions between the individual and the race, between liberty and authority, between mercy and justice, between what is Caesar's and what is God's. Third, proceeding from joint effects of the first two, it comprises traditions of individualism, of limitations on the state, of social responsibility, of revolt and revolution. Fourth, likewise proceeding from the others, particularly from the Christian tradition, it includes a tradition of expansiveness, of missionary and crusading zeal, which has inspired not merely a spasmodic but a steady pushing outward of European frontiers — from the Mediterranean to the Arctic and across the Atlantic, in turn over lands of Celts, Germans, Slavs, Magyars, and Scandinavians, over the full width of both American continents, and beyond to the Philippines and Australasia and into Africa.

In all these characteristics of European or Western civilization, every nationality of central and western Europe and of

[7] Ross Hoffman, "Europe and the Atlantic Community," *Thought*, XX (March, 1945), 25. See also his *The Great Republic* (New York, 1942) and *Durable Peace* (New York, 1944).

America shares. In measure as the frontier advances and is civilized, it is these characteristics which actuate and are embodied in the civilization. The United States is no exception.

One does not have to go to Athens and Rome to behold Greek and Roman architecture, or to Palestine and Europe to see Jewish synagogues and Christian churches. There are more churches and synagogues in the United States than in any other country in the world. There is more classical architecture in Leningrad or London than in Athens, and still more in Washington. It is indeed the practically official architecture of our American democracy from Jefferson to Hoover, and the favorite style for bank buildings, railway stations, and public schools, whether in Virginia or Illinois or the Far West. Our prevailing language continues to be transatlantic English, and distinctively American only in pronunciation and raciness of idiom. Shakespeare and Milton are as much ours as England's. Our juristic conceptions and legal usages are likewise transatlantic, and I know of no philosophical speculation on this continent, in the whole gamut from the pragmatic to the Thomistic, or on any subject from theological to scientific, including political and economic, which has not had its equivalent and usually its antecedent in Europe.

If we belonged to a Moslem or Confucian culture, or to a purely indigenous one, we would not have the mores which we have. We would not, for instance, be free on Sundays for church or golf or for surreptitious privacy in library or laboratory. Probably we would not use knives and forks, and we would wear different clothes. We might be more ceremonial and more externally polite. We might think, as well as behave, differently. Our

sense of values and our frames of reference could not be quite the same. We are what we are only in part because of biological heredity and physical environment. In larger part it is because we are stamped from infancy with a historic culture of singularly educative and perduring potency. . . .

The student of the history of the United States, whether dealing with its political, economic, or cultural development, would be the better historian and the more enlightening if he was a specialist also in the history of a foreign country from which comparisons and contrasts could be drawn. Similarly, the student of the history of a foreign country could profitably extend his study beyond that country. Most of all, the historian of a particular phenomenon, such as nationalism, slavery, democracy, the frontier, etc., however specific in time or space may be his immediate work, must needs possess, if his work is to be informed and judicious, a wide background of acquaintance with other and comparable examples of the phenomenon.

In summary, the American frontier is a frontier of European or "Western" culture. This culture, however modified by or adapted to peculiar geographical and social conditions in America or elsewhere, is still, in essential respects, the culture and hence a continuous bond of the regional community of nations on both sides of the Atlantic. Like its predecessor and inspirer, the Mediterranean community of ancient times, the Atlantic community has been an outstanding fact and a prime factor of modern history. Despite the growth in latter years of an anarchical nationalism and isolationism on one hand, and of a utopian universalism on the other, the Atlantic community has lost none of its potential importance for us and for the world. We must look anew to it and strengthen our ties with it, if we are to escape the tragedy of another world war and ensure the blessings of liberty and democracy to future generations. To this end the historical guild in America can immeasurably contribute by extending the use of the comparative method, by emphasizing the continuity of history, and by stressing cultural and social, equally with political and economic, history.

Avery Craven: FREDERICK JACKSON TURNER

FREDERICK Jackson Turner wrote less and influenced his own generation more than any other important historian. In his lifetime he published only two books, and one of these was a collection of essays already once printed in periodicals.[1] Since his death two other volumes have appeared: one unfinished, and edited by former students; and the other a second collection of previously published essays.[2] Yet one critic has asserted that for forty years Turner "has so completely dominated American historical writing that hardly a single production of that time has failed to show the marks of his influence."[3] Another has insisted that "American history has been reinterpreted and rewritten because of him."[4]

The explanation is simple. It is found in a wealth of suggestive ideas packed into short essays which interpret rather than narrate, and in a stimulating personality which stirred students to curiosity and inspired them to independent research. Turner was both a "first-class mind" and a great teacher.

The thing of first significance in Turner's work was the approach. Until his appearance American historians were, with few exceptions, primarily interested in politics and constitutional problems. Few essayed interpretation. The germ theory of politics, as expounded by Herbert B. Adams, at Johns Hopkins, where Turner went for graduate work, held that American institutions were but a continuation of European beginnings. Economic and social foundations were slighted; geographic factors, largely ignored. American history was a barren waste already sufficiently explored.[5]

Against such attitudes Turner revolted. A Wisconsin background enabled him to take a more penetrating view. He could enter by the back door. Because he had been part of a rapidly changing order, he saw American history as a huge stage on which men, in close contact with raw nature, were ever engaged in the evolution of society from simple beginnings to complex ends. Historians had answered "what" long enough; it was time to inquire as to "how" things came about. America, as it then existed, was the product of the interaction of "economic, political and social forces in contact with

[1] *Rise of the New West* ("American Nation Series," Vol. XIV [New York, 1906]); *The Frontier in American History* (New York, 1920). For a bibliography of Turner's work, see Howard W. Odum (ed.), *American Masters of Social Science* (New York, 1927), pp. 310–12, n. 17.

[2] *The United States, 1830–1850* (New York, 1935); *The Significance of Sections in American History* (New York, 1932).

[3] Louis M. Hacker in the *Nation*, July 26, 1933.

[4] Merle E. Curti, in Stuart A. Rice (ed.), *Methods in Social Science* (Chicago, 1931), p. 367.

[5] F. J. Turner to Carl L. Becker, Dec. 16, 1925 (MS).

From *Marcus W. Jernegan Essays in American Historiography*, William T. Hutchinson, ed., copyright 1937 by the University of Chicago Press. Reprinted by permission of the publisher.

peculiar geographic factors."[6] Such an understanding would give a new American history.

These ideas took definite form quite early in Turner's teaching career and reached public expression in a paper presented to the American Historical Association in 1893 on "The Significance of the Frontier in American History." He offered it not as a fixed formula for the interpretation of all that field but as a suggested approach for reinterpretation.[7] He was calling attention to factors which others had neglected. Nor was he dictating results. He was only pointing out the need for research and indicating new approaches which might yield profit. There is nothing dogmatic about any of the conclusions reached. They were tentative. Some of them applied too largely to the middle period of American history, in which he was primarily interested and in which his researches had been carried on, to have universal application. Turner knew this. Yet, because he saw the deeper significance of the process involved, he spoke in broad, general terms. Here "was a huge page in the history of society." The American pioneer was revealing "luminously the course of universal history."[8] Terms from geology crept in naturally; and the

purely local history of isolated communities was lifted, for those with imaginations, to the dignity of social evolution. One listener, at least, sensed the fact that "the Monroe Doctrine of American historical writing" was being pronounced.

The basic idea developed in this essay, and repeated in later ones with variations and additions, was that American history, through most of its course, presents a series of recurring social evolutions in diverse geographic areas as a people advance to colonize a continent. The chief characteristic is expansion; the chief peculiarity of institutions, constant readjustment. The areas successively occupied differed in the beginning as greatly from each other in physical make-up and resources as did those in Europe which were separated by national lines. They were all wilderness in character, and each in turn represented "the hinter edge of free land." Into these raw and differing areas men and institutions and ideas poured from older basins, there to return to a more or less primitive state and then to climb slowly back toward complexity along lines fixed by the new environments, the old patterns imported, and the accidents of separate evolution. The process was similar in each case, with some common results but always with "essential differences" due to time and place. The final result, as area after area was occupied from the Atlantic to the Pacific, was the Americanization of both men and institutions in the sense that they were better adjusted to their environments and had altered their original character.

The constant re-exposure of things American to a process of "beginning over again" and developing toward urban-industrial conditions made the great West "the true point of view in the his-

---

[6] Turner to Becker, Oct. 3, 1925; Jan. 21, 1911 (MSS).

[7] Turner to Constance L. Skinner, Mar. 18, 1922, *Wisconsin Magazine of History*, XIX (September, 1935), 91–103. Turner, *The Frontier in American History*, p. 3. "This paper makes no attempt to treat the subject exhaustively; its aim is simply to call attention to the frontier as a fertile field for investigation and to suggest some of the problems which arise in connection with it." He had presented his general theses locally before presentation to the American Historical Association.

[8] *The Frontier in American History*, p. 11.

tory of this nation."[9] And because the place of most rapid change was on the outer edge, Turner centered attention there. He did not intend to ignore the more advanced stages in the process or to minimize their significance. He objected sharply to being considered "primarily a western historian"; and once, after calling attention to the fact that "urban development has always been one of those processes," he expressed regret that he could not "start all over and investigate more in detail the eastern aspects."[10] But he did realize that the first steps in shifting the interest of the American historian from the "germ theory of politics" to the new approach must be taken by emphasizing the frontier stage. There the interaction of all forces — geographic, economic, and political — appeared in exaggerated form. There the process by which American society had evolved could best be studied. He would bring the frontier into American history as a sober contributing factor, not as merely a series of romantic episodes. He would place the cowboy, the miner, the pioneer farmer, in proper relations with "big business" and city slums.

With the process and its stages briefly described and the importance of the frontier suggested, Turner enlarged upon the general effects of the latter on American institutions and character. He believed that nationalism and democracy were both promoted and given a peculiarly American flavor by the West and that the individual who lived under its influence acquired new intellectual traits. A coarse strength, a masterful grasp of material things, a restless, buoyant individualism — these and other qualities

[9] *Ibid.*, p. 3.

[10] Turner to Becker, May 14, 1927 (MS).

characterized those who had experienced frontier living.

The statement of these effects was in general terms. Turner used the word "frontier" in loose fashion. Sometimes it referred to a place where men were scarce and nature abundant; again it referred to the process itself and included more than one west. He used the terms "democracy" and "nationalism" in equally indefinite fashion. Seldom was he dealing with a specific geographic area. His interest was in the effects of men and environments on each other, and exact definition was not required.

But it was these general effects which appealed to the imagination of most students, and some came to consider them the basic content of the "Turner thesis." They were applied strictly to definite times and places as universal rules. The American experience was unique. Everything about the frontier made for nationalism and democracy. All frontiersmen were rugged individualists, confirmed idealists, and persistent innovators. The all-important matter of the process was forgotten, and the way opened for distortion and misunderstanding. Most of the later criticism of Turner's work has come for such reasons. Hence, because some students, as Turner once sadly remarked, have "apprehended only certain aspects" of his work and have not always seen "them in *relation*," it is necessary to enlarge somewhat upon his own conception of the bearing of the frontier on nationalism and democracy.

As has been said, Turner stated, after describing the American social process, that the frontier promoted the formation of a composite nationality for the American people. Immigrants were Americanized, and dependence on Europe ended by removal to "the edge of civilization." Frontier problems, growing out of the need for land, ways to market, and markets themselves, developed the national government's powers. Men in a wilderness asked for and secured national protection and aid. "The economic and social characteristics of the frontier worked against sectionalism," and "the mobility of population [was] death to localism."[11]

All this seems strangely contradictory to Turner's own later study of sections in American history and his recognition of the fact that they were produced by the steady flow of peoples out of old areas into new physical basins. Here is open conflict of conclusions, and it would be a simple matter to extract statements regarding the effects of the frontier on nationalism from their settings and to offer them as generalizations easily refuted. In fact, they can be made to appear ridiculous. Yet Turner went on insisting on the nationalizing force of the frontier and describing the thoroughly sectional character of its results.

The matter grows more serious with the second frontier contribution — what it gave to democracy. As described, it was in part individualism, as manifested in opposition to outside oppression or even interference, and in part the greater recognition of individual worth in a wider franchise. But, whatever its character, "it came out of the American forest, and it gained new strength each time it touched a new frontier."[12] Born of contact with free land, it was translated into economic competency and through that into political power. The spoils of office and the right of exploitation for economic advancement were concrete evidence of its immediate application. The pressure put on older sections — even on Europe — by opportunity

opened and escape offered, spread the new freedom and the new equality to common men everywhere. The frontier made real that which was elsewhere too often only a theory.

And yet Turner states clearly that "each new tier of states . . . found in the older ones material for its constitutions." They did not draw them down out of the air. They were not necessarily democratic. Furthermore, the whole social-process idea implied the continuity of the basic elements of American life not only with those on the American seaboard but with those in Europe as well. All things did not begin over again on each frontier in a democratic way. Turner certainly recognized the contributions made to American democracy by the Reformation and by the Puritan revolt at the very moment when he was insisting that it was not carried in the "Susan Constant" to Virginia or in the "Mayflower" to Plymouth. He traced the spread of human slavery from old to new regions, there to become more fixed in a stratified western society, and still talked of a growing democracy. He pointed out the hostility of western men to governmental interference and then told of the tendency among frontiersmen on the plains and in the semiarid regions to call on the central government to do things for them which did violence to all laissez faire attitudes. He emphasized the barnraising, the husking bee, the logrolling, and the neighborhood roundup as normal co-operative efforts among those he depicted as extreme individualists. Everywhere there is contradiction; everywhere conflicting facts which upset sweeping generalizations.

These seemingly conflicting attitudes have puzzled those who did not sit as students in Turner's classes. And they have caused one critic, more clever than

11 *The Frontier in American History*, p. 30.
12 *Ibid.*, p. 293.

wise, to declare "this extraordinary collection of learning . . . quite worthless"
— yes, positively harmful. He has insisted that a mere statement of Turner's
ideas is enough to refute them.[13]

It is not possible to remove completely
all these difficulties. Those who knew the
man and his work at first hand were
seldom conscious of contradictions. They
are even yet a bit resentful, if not con-
temptuous, of those who, lacking the

---

[13] Hacker, *Nation*, CXXXVII, 108–10. Mr.
Hacker has been the most rabid and the least
understanding of Turner's critics. His chief com-
plaints are against Turner's insistence on the
uniqueness of America's historical experience and
on Turner's failure to view all American history
in terms of a class struggle. Turner was talking
about one end of a social experience; Hacker has
his eyes fixed on the other end. The constant exposure of institutions to the influence of free land
on a frontier was a unique experience in national
history. The urban-industrial complexity reached
at the end of the whole process of evolution from
raw frontier simplicity is not unique. Viewed,
say, with the eyes of east side New York in 1930,
American conditions would not appear to differ
from those of the Old World. The class struggle
probably would appear to be the chief thing toward which American life had ever been moving.
The farmer would appear only as a much abused
victim of capitalistic greed. But there are unique
elements in that situation which have come into
it through the process by which it has been
reached. The attitudes of all groups differ a bit
from those in other mature social units. The
weapons they use and the way they are used have
an American flavor. The rugged individualism of
the frontier is still something to conjure with. The
American farmer is still far from a peasant in
temper regardless of material conditions. The
American millionaire has acted in a rather unique
way with his millions. The democratic dogma is
something even yet quite distinct from European
democracy as it rises out of the great rural American regions. The average American is still far
more sectionally conscious than he is class conscious. And American history must avoid a completely urban-industrial viewpoint if it is to
remain true to the facts of two centuries and more
of rural dominance. The process by which we
reached complexity is still more significant as a
historical fact than the mere conditions reached
at the end of that process. See reviews in *ibid.*,
July 26, 1933, and the *New Republic*, June 5,
1935.

memory of a mind which could master
detail and then rise far above mere facts
to illuminate the whole in universal setting, fail to grasp the real meaning of
Turner's work. They forget that something passed with the man — something
essential to understanding. Turner dis-
solved petty contradictions in the very
breadth of his grasp. His ceaseless curiosity gave objectivity; his open-minded-
ness forbade dogmatism. He moved so
swiftly from one station to another, that
he passed by, though not unconsciously,
much that employs lesser minds. He ab-
horred generalizations, as many a graduate student learned to his sorrow; but
he himself wrote the kind of history
which required generalizations. It was
never a narrative of successive events,
but rather Turner's own understanding
of the meaning in events. Separated from
the man himself and his wider work, or
given over for application to students
who do not comprehend their full meaning, those generalizations become as
weak and as dangerous as generalizations have a reputation of being. It is
not strange that there have been both
criticism and misunderstanding. Even at
the expense of some repetition, a closer
examination of Turner's own statements
should be made. Limits for their application should be set.

The unity in Turner's work and the
key to its real significance, if there is such
a key, is found in the approach already
noticed. Turner spoke of it as "changes
in perspective." He was interested in
explaining the United States of his day
by its history, as revealed in the "inter-
relations of economics, politics, sociology, culture in general, with geographic
factors." He began with *things as they
were* and asked how they came to be
as they were.[14]

---

[14] Turner to Becker, Oct. 3, 1925 (MS).

Most historians, as has been said, had answered in terms of old-world germs continuing development in the new. Turner understood the "crossroads society" of the Middle West well enough to realize that men there would not agree. They thought of themselves as unique, and of their experiment in democracy as a sharp departure from all that lay across the Atlantic. And he agreed in as far as historical perspective permitted. He knew full well the heritage with which America began — men and institutions; hopes, fears, prejudices, and ideals. Most of the social and intellectual patterns had been and still were basically those taken first from Europe and then from older regions in our own East. But something new had crept in. European travelers sensed a new flavor in Boston and Philadelphia and on the farms 'round about. The outlook was different, even the temper. They spoke of more independence in men, of more hope and of more social-economic achievement. The traveler from the American East felt the same difference when he visited the new "Wests." Something American was being added. Changes were being wrought here slowly, there more rapidly. A people on the move, a society fluid in quality, men and institutions thrown in successive waves against the forest and plains, were taking on, in different geographic areas, a *native* tone, if not form.[15]

Turner, in attempting to explain his United States, emphasized these differences — refined out the American qualities and explained their origins in terms of the process by which society had developed in the American physical regions. It was a society of contradictions

— the very democratic dogma, which was its boast, was composed of both liberty and equality — things hostile to the point of destroying each other. A raw life fading irregularly back into urban-industrial complexity presented every variety of interest and every stage through which mankind in its long toil up the course of civilization had experienced. Crosscurrents of every kind appeared in the stream of national life. Sometimes they ran opposite to the general current. The intense pressure for labor in the conquest of a continent brought slavery into a society fundamentally democratic in practice and profession. The very physical character of the tasks to be done made men, who were at heart idealists, coarse and practical and materially minded. Preoccupation with the pressing work of making a living forced the borrowing of social and political institutions from older states in the East by men prone to innovation, with the consequent restriction of more liberal forms, at least for a time. Every quality manifested had somewhere its opposite. Even the national life seemed often to drift rather than move ahead. There were too many conflicting interests, too many confused demands. And a babel of voices, in a government of majorities, could not command a straight course. Sections differing in age, in physical resources and environments, in origins of settlers, institutions, and values held, could only move forward by compromise. And compromise does not give clear-cut, positive direction.

If, by careful survey and comparison of frontiers and "Wests," Turner found a drift toward "democracy and nationalism," he had reference not to sharp, well-defined, all-inclusive qualities but rather to general tendencies which stood out amid contradictions and variations but

[15] Joseph Schafer, *Wisconsin Magazine of History*, XVI (June, 1933), 451–69; *ibid.*, XVII (June, 1934), 447–65.

which were, nevertheless, easily distinguished and universally recognized. And their importance was enhanced by their very failure to yield to exactness in application. Turner's democracy manifested itself more in the erect head, the stubborn jaw, the buoyant spirit of confidence, the faith in "King Numbers," the sharp dislike of privilege, and the insistence on unrestricted opportunity than in any violent recasting of institutions. These were the things which the traveler noticed. These were the things which led to a wider franchise when the settlers "got 'round" to it. In the meantime the democratic dogma might be employed in defending those who had stolen a "quarter section" of land from the government. Such democracy cannot be comprehended by a comparison of western state constitutions with those of the coast, because all American constitutions, of coast and interior alike, have felt the force of the frontier, and because the very process of American institutional development was one of borrowing and later adjusting, not creating. To require a frontier, strictly defined as two persons to the square mile, to make for itself either political or social institutions without reference to habit and origins is absurd. To test the soundness of Turner's belief in the frontier as a democratizing force by such a requirement is even a greater absurdity.[16]

Turner himself adequately revealed the contradictions of frontier nationalism by his work on the sections.[17] But he did not repudiate it. A national outlook of a certain kind among western

[16] See Benjamin F. Wright, Jr., "Political Institutions and the Frontier," in D. R. Fox (ed.), *Sources of Culture in the Middle West* (New York, 1934), pp. 15–38; also *Yale Review*, XX, 349–65.

[17] *Sections in American History, passim; The Rise of the New West; The United States, 1830–1850.* It should be noticed that Turner's two

men was too obvious, even though the crosscurrents ran in quite a different direction. No one would deny that the rising West turned the eyes of Americans inland for several generations, made commerce largely internal instead of foreign, and built lines of communication between distant units to forward that trade. No one could question the fact that internal problems occupied the American statesmen for decades after the War of 1812. Nor could they ignore the larger interest in central government manifested by those who, having left the states of their nativity behind, now looked toward Washington for protection and aid in "advancing civilization." From that angle they could readily agree that the frontier "worked against sectionalism." But they would be blind, indeed, if they did not recognize the fact that the development of distinct and potentially hostile sections might be wrapped up in the very process of westward expansion. Turner pointed this out and made sectionalism the dominant interest of his later studies. He insisted that the occupation of geographic provinces and the evolution of society in them made American history in its later stages largely the record of sectional conflict, sectional combinations, and sectional compromises. When compromise failed, war was a danger and, in one case, a reality. Newer areas demanded peculiar legislation in the treatment of the public domain, the building of internal improvements, the handling of finances, and the encouragement of markets. The older ones required other policies. Northern interests sometimes ran counter to those of the South; mining or manufacturing demands often opposed those of agricul-

volumes of history are, after all, sectional studies —the national side of the story, which follows sectional analysis, being largely the interplay of sectional forces.

ture. Even diplomacy had to consider the conflicting claims of different sections. The American statesman, under such conditions, tended to become a sectional spokesman, and "democracy" and "nationalism" were often only emotional stimulants called in to add force to sectional demands. The clash of economic interests closely associated with regional geography gives to American life something of the European international flavor. We are in one sense a federation of "potential nations." The very fact that we have, by discussion and compromise, largely avoided violence, Turner thought, revealed the possibility of "international political parties, international legislative bodies, and international peace."

Nor did Turner neglect the social implications in the evolutionary approach he had taken. Much of the misunderstanding of his work could be avoided by a reading of the essay on "Social Forces in American History" in connection with that on the frontier.[18] The one is a corollary of the other, and almost as important. In this essay Turner faced the problems of American life "when the West was gone" and when urban-industrial complexity predominated. He saw the problems produced by a continuation of the ruthless individualism which the frontier had bred and by the thrusting of frontier attitudes into a new social order which they could neither comprehend nor control. By 1910, when he spoke, "world-wide forces of reorganization incident to the age of steam production and large-scale industry" were writing a new and "wonderful chapter" in American life. The industrial revolution, not the frontier end of the American process, was shaping society. The old isolation was gone. The United States was in world-politics. Natural resources had largely passed into private hands. For-

eign labor crowded our shores, and concentrated wealth gave the keeping of the many into the hands of the few. "Self-made . . . coal barons, steel kings, oil kings, railroad magnates, masters of capital and monarchs of trusts" championed the old pioneer individualism as against the efforts at social control. They arrayed the ideal of freedom in the democratic dogma against its fellow-ideal of equality. A government-of-the-people's struggle for social justice was being thwarted by the continued emphasis on, and worship of, qualities suited only to a pioneer agricultural order. Class conflict was taking the place of geographic sectionalism. American ideals were demanding readjustment to fit the new conditions of a day when the frontier was gone.

Turner concluded that the tangled situation presented could be grasped only by "an understanding of the rise and progress of the forces which . . . made it . . . ," and insisted that "we should rework our history from the new points of view afforded by the present." The time had come to place larger stress on that phase of the American social process which lay at the other end from the frontier.[19]

Turner was, of course, a careful, scholarly craftsman in spite of the fact that he undoubtedly viewed history as an art rather than as a science.[20] He laboriously, yet joyously, gathered materials and carefully weighed and analyzed them. His files were filled with countless pages of statistics. The votes of congressmen on measures of all kinds were compiled and plotted on charts and maps. He was never ready for final judgment while sources remained unworked. He was ever ready to forsake the painful task of writing in order to follow up some

18 *The Frontier in American History*, pp. 311–34.

19 *Ibid.*

20 See Curti, *loc. cit.,* pp. 355–62.

new clue or to digest some new document. He once said of himself: "I am not philosopher enough to be a 'maker of social sciences' — but I have had a lot of fun exploring, getting lost and getting back, and telling my companions about it."[21] His favorite poem was Kipling's "The Explorer."

The most vital thing in Turner's method was the wide character of materials on which he drew. "Literature and art, politics, economics, sociology, psychology, biology and physiography" all furnished data. He brought all these into larger cooperation in his work, and each of these fields is indebted to him for scholarly service. He was a historian both of the oldest and newest schools.

One lasting impression which the student carried away from Turner's classes and from his workshop was that of countless maps, jigsaw in appearance, because they represented the plotting of votes by counties. Such graphic representation revealed sectional interests, the force of habit, the persistence of viewpoint carried by migrants from older areas into newer ones. When thrown against geological survey maps, racial maps, or cultural maps of various kinds, they added something to the American story not to be found elsewhere. Turner gave the United States census maps a new place in the historian's equipment. By his work the character of map materials used in history books was to a degree, at least, altered for the better.

Much attention has been given by writers to the origins of the Turner frontier thesis.[22] He made no claim to priority but insisted on the independent character of his own formulation. To the inquiry of writers he went back to a boyhood in Wisconsin where bits of the old frontier still persisted. He had hunted and fished along rivers where Indian tepees still were to be found. The raftsmen from the pineries sometimes "tied up" at his town. New Englanders, southerners, Germans, Scotchmen, Welshmen, Irishmen, and Scandinavians, mingled together in this "mixing bowl." The local politicians met in his father's newspaper office. He saw democracy painfully at work. And under his very eye Wisconsin left pioneer days behind. At the state university Professor William F. Allen taught him "the ideals of scholarship," and Draper permitted him to work with a rich collection of fur-trader manuscripts. At Johns Hopkins the emphasis on European institutions and the neglect of geographic factors and western influence in American history turned him back to his own experiences as a truer approach to the story.[23] Others had already caught something of the importance of the frontier factors in American life, but Turner gave them full expression at the time when history study in the United States was ready to incorporate them. There is little point in searching out earlier statements which recognize the social process but which did not take hold to influence the study of American history. But if it is to be done, this terse paragraph from the pen of Thomas Jefferson deserves more attention than it has received:

Let a philosophic observer commence a journey from the savages of the Rocky Mountains, eastwardly toward our seacoast. These [the Indians] he would observe in the earliest stage of association living under no law but that of nature, subsisting and covering themselves with the flesh and skins of wild beasts. He would next find these on our frontiers in the pastoral state, raising domestic animals to

[21] Turner to Becker, Feb. 13, 1926 (MS).

[22] H. C. Nixon, "Precursors of Turner in the Interpretation of the American Frontier," *South Atlantic Quarterly*, January, 1929.

[23] Turner to Becker, Dec. 16, 1925 (MS).

supply the defects of hunting. Then succeed to our own semibarbarous citizens, the pioneers of the advance civilization, and so in his progress he would meet the gradual shades of an improving man until he would reach his, as yet, most improved state in our seaport towns. This, in fact, is equivalent to a survey, in time, of the progress of man from the infancy of creation, to the present day.[24]

In this connection, also, it must be remembered that Turner's protest against the historian's neglect of the West coincided with the Populist's demand for larger political recognition of western interests and with William Jennings Bryan's redefinition of the term "business man" so as to include the western farmer. Each of these spokesmen, whether politician or historian, was, in a way, reaffirming faith in the old individualistic democracy which now faced the advancing urban-industrial order. All revealed, in differing degrees, a crusading flavor. All looked backward, rather than forward, for values. All manifested a supreme confidence in the basic soundness of the "American experiment" as it had been and an equal distrust of the new forces which moved to dominance. Turner's strength, as well as his weakness — yes, even the appeal his writings made to his own generation — can be understood, in part at least, only by the fact that his work was an expression of the American mind and spirit at "the turn of the century."

The work which came from Turner's own pen is poor measure of his contribution to American scholarship. No other historian of the day inspired in others so much original investigation. Never particularly interested in teaching per se, he thereby became a great teacher. He

once begged a former student, who was writing a sketch of him, not to hand him "down to posterity as a teacher." "I had no interest in the 'shooting' of the young idea," he said, "I was interested in history, and in the companionship of men like yourself."[25] And that was exactly what made him "a master." He shared his field with those who had the capacity to appreciate it. He stimulated their interests. His eager mind saw opportunities for new investigation amid the welter of forces which his conception of history implied, and the task was "too big for one investigator and one historian." Students might become companions on his journeys to this frontier. But he would not "rubber-stamp" their minds. He would only point out a great unoccupied land — a wilderness they might pioneer and claim for scholarship, something "tucked away below the foothills where the trail runs out and stops." He had the explorer's instinct, but he also had the good sense to keep out of the way of those "who were willing to blaze trails of their own."[26]

It is therefore not surprising that Turner's students worked in many fields or that they pioneered many lines. Some contributed to economic and social history on subjects that ranged from agriculture to industry, centered on finances or transportation, on primitive Indian tribes, or on the efforts of mature societies to end wars. Some wrote local history — state or regional. Others dealt with the sections. Diplomatic and political events, well set on their economic foundations, attracted a few. But regardless of the field entered — and they ranged across the whole of America, east and west, north and south, early and late — each believed that he had secured his

24 Thomas Jefferson to William Ludlow, Sept. 16, 1824, Official Papers, *Writings*, XVI, 74–75.

25 Turner to Becker, Nov. 23, 1925 (MS); Turner to A. O. Craven, Nov. 20, 1926 (MS). 26 *Ibid.*

inspiration and his start from Frederick Jackson Turner.[27]

It is always difficult to write of this man in an impersonal way. He "inspired affection as well as admiration." The rich quality of his voice, the kindly twinkle of his eye, the genuine modesty in regard to achievements, the keen humor of lasting quality — these things and many others have been spoken of by loyal students. But there was something more which Turner possessed and which others caught from him that can be explained only in personal terms. Few who write of him escape the pressure for "personal testimony." I may as well succumb now as later, not for the purpose of telling about myself but to reveal something of Turner which can be conveyed in no other way. I went to Harvard with only the quantity of history I had been unable to resist in a small western college. I left Turner's classes after a year of work, eager and willing to study the history of one county in a rural state. Its hills and valleys had become for me a stage on which a great epic in human history had been written. Its early settlers were part of a great trek; its slow rise from a wilderness to the complexity of general farming about a county seat of four thousand souls was part of a great national and international process. The old buffalo wallows in a prairie stretch and the old abandoned flour mills on its muddy streams were one with the small factories of the town which accepted them as the first steps to industrial importance. The old news-

[27] A list of Turner's students who have made real contributions to history is given in Curti, *loc. cit.*, pp. 359–67. It is, however, not complete. Turner influenced fellow-workers in the field of American history also, and gave suggestions which others, who never felt his personal touch, carried out. Few men received more reprints from authors, and no one is mentioned as often in authors' prefaces. Truly he did influence a whole generation of writers.

papers and family letters in the attic were social documents. I could be a historian by knowing all about this one area, because local history was human history. Of course the outlook changed with greater maturity; but the interest in all social-economic-political matters, the fear of being too certain about things, and the unrest as long as more could be learned, remained as something of an obligation for having "worked with Turner." He did that to most of us.

The historian is the child of his age. New shifts in interests alter values and outlooks. History must be re-written by each generation for itself. It would be asking too much that Turner be to another generation what he was to his own. It is probably fair to say that he generalized too much for the whole West from the Old Northwest which he knew so well. He may have insisted a bit more on the uniqueness of the American experience than the facts warranted, and he may not have stressed the industrial-agricultural class conflicts enough — but this is doubtful. His faith in America's future may have been too great, his hope for democracy too high. These were common faults in his day. But the questions he asked are more or less permanent ones for those who would know how America came to be what it is. His answers may not exactly fit when the pattern is entirely unfolded. He would be among those greatly surprised if they did. I one time asked him why he did not answer a critic who had distorted in order to criticize. He only chuckled and said: "I've always been surprised that there has not been more of criticism." He was too eager for truth to care for praise or blame. He was running down a new clue on Calhoun when death interrupted the eternal urge to "go and look behind the ranges."

Walter Prescott Webb:

THE FRONTIER AND THE 400 YEAR BOOM

I

SINCE America led the way in evolving the frontier process, and leads the world in the study of that process, we have no choice but to examine the American experience and to note briefly how scholars came to attend it as a field of study. American historians assume that the frontier process began with the English settlement at Jamestown in 1607, and the year 1890 is usually taken to mark the date when there was no more frontier available, when the new land was no longer new. There may be some quibbling about the dates, but they do bracket the three centuries of American frontier experience and experimentation.

It was the magnitude and the unbroken continuity of the experience that gave the frontier major importance in American life. It made no difference what other tasks the Americans had on their hands at a given time, there was the additional, ever-present one of moving into and settling new country. They did it while they fought for independence, before and after; they did it while they hammered out the principles of a democratic government shaped to the needs of frontiersmen; and they did not cease doing it in the period of civil strife. They never reached the limits of the vacancy they owned before they acquired another vacancy, by purchase, by treaty, by conquest, and in every case the frontiersmen infiltrated the country before the nation acquired it. Like locusts they swarmed, always to the west, and only the Pacific Ocean stopped them. Here in this movement beat the deep overtone of a nation's destiny, and to it all kept step unconsciously.

To say that the people were unconscious of the force that moved them, and of the medium in which they moved, is to state a fact which is easy to prove but hard to explain. It may be said that they were emotionally aware of the frontier long before they were intellectually cognizant of it. People could not have as their main task for three centuries working with raw land without getting its dirt under their nails and deep into their skins. The effects were everywhere, in democratic government, in boisterous politics, in exploitative agriculture, in mobility of population, in disregard for conventions, in rude manners, and in unbridled optimism. Though these effects were present everywhere they were not understood anywhere by the people who felt and reflected them. The frontier still lacked its philosopher, the thinker who could view the whole dramatic experience and tell what was its meaning. This philosopher arrived three years after the experience ended and told the American

From Walter Prescott Webb, "Ended: 400 Year Boom, Reflections on the Age of the Frontier," *Harper's Magazine*, Vol. CCIII (October, 1951), 26–33. Reprinted by permission.

people that from the beginning the American frontier had been the dominant force, the determining factor, in their history thus far.

This hypothesis was presented to the American Historical Association in a paper entitled "The Significance of the Frontier in American History." The date was 1893 and the author was a young and then little-known historian. That paper made Frederick Jackson Turner a scholar with honor in his own country; it altered the whole course of American historical scholarship, and it is recognized as the most influential single piece of historical writing ever done in the United States. The key to his thesis is found in this sentence: "The existence of an area of free land, its continuous recession, and the advance of American settlement westward, explain American development." The general acceptance of this frontier hypothesis, and the fame of its author, came about because the people in America were emotionally prepared to understand this rationalization and explanation of their own long experience. Turner's pupils — many of whom became disciples — flocked to the diggings and have worked out in every cove and valley the rich vein which he uncovered, but not one of them, not even the master himself, took the next step to point out or at least to emphasize that the American frontier was but a small fragment of the Great Frontier. On that Great Frontier was also an area of free land; it was in continuous recession; and the advance of European settlement into it should explain the development of Western civilization in modern times just as the American advance explains American development.

II

What happened in America was but a detail in a much greater phenomenon, the interaction between European civilization and the vast raw lands into which it moved. An effort will be made here to portray the whole frontier, to suggest how it affected the life and institutions of Western civilization throughout the modern period; and as a basis for this exposition four propositions are submitted for consideration:

(1) Europe had a frontier more than a century before the United States was settled.

(2) Europe's frontier was much greater than that of the United States, or of any other one nation; it was the greatest of all time.

(3) The frontier of Europe was almost, if not quite, as important in determining the life and institutions of modern Europe as the frontier of America was in shaping the course of American history. Without the frontier modern Europe would have been so different from what it became that it could hardly be considered modern at all. This is almost equivalent to saying that the frontier made Europe modern.

(4) The close of the Great Frontier may mark the end of an epoch in Western civilization just as the close of the American frontier is often said to have marked the end of the first phase of American history. If the close of the Great Frontier does mark the end of an age, the modern age, then the institutions designed to function in a society dominated largely by frontier forces will find themselves under severe strain.

If we conceive of Western Europe as a unified, densely populated region with a common culture and civilization — which it has long had basically — and if we see the frontier also as a unit, a vast and vacant land without culture, we are in position to view the interaction between the two as a simple but gigantic operation extending over more than four centuries, a process that may appear to be the drama of modern civilization.

To emphasize the unity of western Europe, and at the same time set it off in sharp contrast to its opposite, the frontier, we may call it the Metropolis. Metropolis is a good name, implying what Europe really was, a cultural center holding within it everything pertaining to Western civilization. Prior to 1500 the Metropolis comprised all the "known" world save Asia, which was but vaguely known. Its area was approximately 3,750,000 square miles, and its population is estimated to have been about 100 million people.

There is no need to elaborate the conditions under which these people lived, but it should be remembered that by modern standards the society was a static one with well-defined classes. The population pressed hard on the means of subsistence. There was not much food, practically no money, and very little freedom. What is more important, there was practically no means of escape for those people living in this closed world. The idea of progress had not been born. Heaven alone, which could be reached only through the portals of death, offered any hope to the masses of the Metropolis.

Then came the miracle that was to change everything, the emancipator bearing rich gifts of land and more land, of gold and silver, of new foods for every empty belly and new clothing stuffs for every half-naked back. Europe, the Metropolis, knocked on the door of the Great Frontier, and when the door was opened it was seen to be golden, for within there was undreamed-of treasure, enough to make the whole Metropolis rich. The long quest of a half-starved people had at last been rewarded with success beyond comprehension.

Columbus has been accepted as the symbol, as the key that unlocked the golden door to a new world, but we know that he was only one of a group of curious investigators, Portuguese, Spanish, English, Dutch, and Scandinavian, men of the Metropolis and not of one country. Within a brief period, as history is told, Columbus and his prying associates pulled back the curtains of ignorance and revealed to the Metropolis three new continents, a large part of a fourth, and thousands of islands in oceans hitherto hardly known. They brought all of these — continents, oceans, and islands — and deposited them as a free gift at the feet of the impoverished Metropolis.

The Metropolis had a new piece of property and the frontier had a new owner. The Metropolitans were naturally curious about their property, and quite naturally began to ask questions about it. How big is it? Who lives on it? What is its inherent worth? What can *I* get out of it? They learned that the frontier had an area five or six times that of Europe; that it was practically vacant, occupied by a few primitive inhabitants whose rights need not be respected; that its inherent worth could only be guessed at. As to what can *I* get out of it?, the answer came in time clear and strong: You can get everything you want from gold and silver to furs and foods, and in any quantity you want, provided only that you are willing to venture and work! And more faintly came the small voice, hardly audible: Something all of you can get as a by-product is some measure of freedom.

The Metropolitans decided to accept the gifts. Instantly the divisions in Europe were projected into the frontier as each little European power that could man a ship seized a section of the frontier bigger than itself and tried to fight all the others off. Each nation wanted it all. The result was a series of wars lasting from 1689 to 1763 and from these wars England, France, and Spain emerged as chief owners of the frontier world. Their success was more apparent than real, for a spirit of freedom had been nurtured in the distant lands, and in less than fifty years England had lost her chief prize while Spain and France had lost practically everything.

But their loss, like their previous gain, was more apparent than real. True, by 1820 the Metropolis had lost title to most of the new land, but it had not lost something more precious than title — namely, the beneficent effects that the frontier exerted on the older countries. The political separation of most of North and South America relieved the Metropolis of responsibility and onerous obligations, but it did not cut off the abundance of profits. Europe continued to share in the riches and the opportunity that the opening of the golden door had made visible.

III

What was the essential character of the frontier? Was the direct force it exerted spiritual, intellectual, or was it material? The frontier was basically a vast body of wealth without proprietors. It was an empty land more than five times the size of western Europe, a land whose resources had not been exploited. Its first impact was mainly economic. Bathed in and invigorated by a flood of wealth, the Metropolis began to seethe with economic excitement.

With all the ships coming and going, the wharves of Europe were piled high with strange goods, the tables were set with exotic foods of delightful flavors, and new-minted coins of gold and silver rattled in the coffers of the market place. The boom began when Columbus re-turned from his first voyage, and it continued at an ever-accelerating pace until the frontier that fed it was no more. Assuming that the frontier closed about 1890, it may be said that the boom lasted approximately four hundred years. It lasted so long that it came to be considered the normal state, a fallacious assumption for any boom. It is conceivable that this boom has given the peculiar character to modern history, to what we call Western civilization.

Assuming that there was such a boom and that it lasted four hundred years, it follows that a set of institutions, economic, political, and social, would in that time evolve to meet the needs of the world in boom. Insofar as they were designed to meet peculiar conditions, these institutions would be specialized boomward. It is accepted that a set of institutions has developed since 1500, and we speak of them as modern to distinguish them from medieval institutions. Therefore we may well inquire whether our modern institutions — economic, political, and social, constituting the superstructure of Western civilization — are founded on boom conditions.

The factors involved, though of gigantic magnitude, are simple in nature and in their relation one to another. They are the old familiar ones of population, land, and capital. With the opening of the Great Frontier, land and capital rose out of all proportion to population, of those to share it, and therefore conditions were highly favorable to general prosperity and a boom. What we are really concerned with is an *excess* of land and an *excess* of capital for division among a relatively *fixed* number of people. The population did increase, but not until the nineteenth century did the extra population compare with the extra land and capital that had been long available.

For example, in 1500 the Metropolis had a population of 100 million people crowded into an area of 3,750,000 square miles. The population density for the entire Metropolis was 26.7 persons per square mile. For each person there was available about twenty-four acres, a ratio that changed little from 1300 to 1650. The opening of the frontier upset the whole situation by destroying the balance that had been struck between land and man. A land excess of nearly 20 million square miles became available to the same number of people, reducing population density to less than five, increasing the average area per individual to 148 acres instead of 24.

Capital may be considered in two forms, as gold and silver and as capital goods or commodities. The Metropolis was short of both forms of wealth throughout the medieval period, and the dearth of coin prior to the discoveries was most critical. It has been estimated that the total amount of gold and silver in Europe in 1492 was less than 200 million dollars, less than two dollars per person. Certainly there was not enough to serve the needs of exchange, which was carried on by barter, or to give rise to erudite theories of money economy. Then very suddenly the whole money situation changed.

By 1500 the Spaniards had cracked the treasure houses of the Great Frontier and set a stream of gold and silver flowing into the Metropolis, a stream that continued without abatement for 150 years, and that still continues. This flood of precious metals changed all the relations existing between man and money, between gold and a bushel of wheat or a *fanega* of barley. That changed relationship wrought the price revolution because temporarily — so fast did the metals come — there was more money than things, and

so prices rose to the modern level. This new money was a powerful stimulus to the quest for more, and set the whole Metropolis into the frenzy of daring and adventure which gave character to the modern age.

Since our concern here is with the excess of wealth over population, we may examine with interest the rise in the quantity of gold and silver. Taking the 200 million dollars of 1492 as a base, we find that by 1600 the amount had increased eightfold, by 1700 it had risen nearly twentyfold, by 1800 it stood at thirty-sevenfold, and by 1900 at a hundred-and-fourfold over what was on hand when the frontier was opened. Obviously this increase of precious metals was out of all proportion to the increase in population. If we grant that an excess of money makes a boom, then here in this new treasure was the stuff a boom needed. It is safe to say that out of each $100 worth of precious metals produced in the world since 1493, not less than $85 have been supplied by the frontier countries and not more than $15 by the Metropolis, including Asia. The bearing of these facts on the rise of a money economy, of modern capitalism, is something for the economists to think about.

The spectacular influx of precious metals should not obscure the fact that they constituted but the initial wave of wealth rolling into the Metropolis from the Great Frontier. Wave followed wave in endless succession in the form of material things, and each deposit left the Metropolis richer than before. Unfortunately the quantity of material goods cannot be measured, but we know it was enormous. South America sent coffee, Africa, cocoa, and the West Indies sent sugar to sweeten them. Strange and flavorsome fruits came from the tropics. From primeval forests came ship timbers, pitch, and tar with which to build the fleets for merchants and warriors. North America sent furs for the rich and cotton for the poor so that all could have more than one garment. The potato, adapted to the Metropolis, became second to bread as the staff of life. The New World gave Indian corn or maize, and the rich lands on which to grow it, and in time hides and beef came from the plains and pampas of two continents. Everywhere in Europe from the royal palace to the humble cottage men smoked American tobacco and under its soothing influence dreamed of far countries, wealth, and adventure. Scientists brought home strange plants and herbs and made plant experiment stations in scores of European gardens. In South America they found the bark of a tree from which quinine was derived to cure malaria and another plant which they sent to the East Indies to establish the rubber industry. No, it is not possible to measure the amount of goods flowing into Europe, but it can be said that the Great Frontier hung for centuries like the horn of plenty over the Metropolis and emptied out on it an avalanche of wealth.

At this point let us turn to the growth of population, the number of people who in a rough sense shared the excess of land and of precious metals. As stated above the population in 1500 stood at about 100 million, and it did not increase appreciably before 1650. All the people of European origin, whether in the Metropolis or in the Great Frontier, had a little more than doubled by 1800. Not until the nineteenth century was the increase rapid. By 1850 the increase was more than threefold, by 1900 more than fivefold, but in 1940 population had increased eightfold over that of 1500. The significant fact is that between 1500 and 1850 the quantity of both land and capital stood high out of all proportion to the quantity of popu-

lation. Equally significant, and somewhat disturbing, is the fact that the excess of land incident to opening the frontier disappeared in the world census of 1930. By 1940 the enlarged Western world was more crowded than the small world of Europe was in 1500. It was the observation of this fact which led Dean Inge to remark in 1938 that "the house is full." Much earlier William Graham Sumner commented on the man-land ratio: "It is this ratio of population to land which determines what are the possibilities of human development or the limits of what man can attain in civilization and comfort." To put the matter in another way, if the boom rested on a four-century excess of land over population, the land base of the boom disappeared in 1930.

The boom hypothesis of modern history may be summed up by stating that with the tapping of the resources of the Great Frontier there came into the possession of the Metropolis a body of wealth consisting of land, precious metals, and commodities out of all proportion to the number of people. . . .

IV

If the opening of the Great Frontier did precipitate a boom in Western civilization, the effects on human ideas and institutions must have been profound and far-reaching. In general such a boom would hasten the passing away of the ideas and institutions of a static culture and the sure appearance of others adapted to a dynamic and prospering society. There is no doubt that medieval society was breaking up at the time of the discoveries, that men's minds had been sharpened by their intellectual exercises, and that their spirits had been stirred by doubt. The thinkers were restless and inquiring, but what they lacked was room in which to try out their innovations, and a fresh and un-cluttered soil in which some of their new ideas could take hold and grow. Their desires had to be matched with opportunity before they could realize on their aspirations, however laudable. The frontier offered them the room and the opportunity. It did not necessarily originate ideas, but it acted as a relentless sifter, letting some pass and rejecting others. Those that the frontier favored prospered, and finally matured into institutions; those it did not favor became recessive, dormant, and many institutions based on these ideas withered away. Feudal tenure, serfdom, barter, primogeniture, and the notion that the world was a no-good place in which to live are examples of things untenable in the presence of the frontier.

Since we are dealing with the modern age, it would be very helpful if we could discover what it emphasized most. Where was the chief accent of modernity? What has been its focus? *Who* has held the spotlight on the stage of history since 1500? There can be little doubt, though there may be enough to start an argument, that the answer to all these questions is: the Individual. It is he who has been emphasized, accented; it is on him that the spotlight has focused; it is his importance that has been magnified. He is — or was — the common denominator of modern times, and an examination of any strictly modern institution such as democracy or capitalism will reveal an individual at the core, trying to rule himself in one case and make some money in the other. Not God nor the devil nor the state, but the ordinary man has been the favorite child of modern history.

Did the Great Frontier, which was his contemporary, have any part in giving the individual his main chance, the triple opportunity of ruling himself, enriching

himself, and saving his own soul on his own hook? These three freedoms were institutionalized in Protestantism, capitalism, and democracy — whose basic assumption is that they exist for the individual, and that the individual must be free in order to make them work. The desire for freedom men surely have always had, but in the old Metropolis conditions prevailed which made freedom impossible. Everywhere in Europe the individual was surrounded by institutions which, whether by design or not, kept him unfree. He was walled in by man-made regulations which controlled him from baptism to extreme unction.

Then the golden door of the Great Frontier opened, and a way of escape lay before him. He moved out from the Metropolis to land on a distant shore, in America, Australia, South Africa. Here in the wild and empty land there was not a single institution; man had left them, albeit temporarily, far behind. Regardless of what befell him later, for an instant he was free of all the restrictions that society had put upon him. In short, he had escaped his human masters only to find himself in the presence of another, a less picayunish one.

The character of the new master, before whom he stood stripped of his institutions, was so in contrast with that of the old one as to defy comparison. Man stood naked in the presence of nature. On this subject, Alexander von Humboldt said, "In the Old World, nations and the distinction of their civilization form the principal point in the picture; in the New World, man and his production almost disappear amidst the stupendous display of wild and gigantic nature." The outstanding qualities of wild and gigantic nature are its impersonality and impassiveness. Nature broods over man, casts its mysterious spells, but it never intervenes for or against him. It gives no orders, issues no proclamations, has no prisons, no privileges; it knows nothing of vengeance or mercy. Before nature all men are free and equal.

The important point is that the abstract man we have been following did not have to *win* his freedom. It was imposed upon him and he could not escape it. Being caught in the trap of freedom, his task was to adjust himself to it and to devise procedures which would be more convenient for living in such a state. His first task was to govern himself, for self-government is what freedom imposes.

Of course there was not just one man on the frontier. In a short time the woods were full of them, all trained in the same school. As the years went by, they formed the habits of freedom, cherished it; and when a distant government tried to take from them that to which they had grown accustomed, they resisted, and their resistance was called the American Revolution. The American frontiersmen did not fight England to gain freedom, but to preserve it and have it officially recognized by the Metropolis. "Your nation," wrote Herman Melville, "enjoyed no little independence before your declaration declared it." Whence came this independence? Not from parliaments or kings or legislative assemblies, but from the conditions, the room, the space, and the natural wealth amidst which they lived. "The land was ours," writes Robert Frost, "before we were the land's."

The other institution that magnified the importance of the individual was capitalism, an economic system under which each person undertakes to enrich himself by his own effort. It is only in the presence of great abundance that such a free-for-all system of wealth-getting can long operate. There must be present enough wealth to go around to

make such an economy practicable. We have seen that the tapping of the frontier furnished just this condition, a superabundance of land, of gold and silver, and of commodities which made the principle of *laissez faire* tenable. In the frontier the embryonic capitalists of the sixteenth and seventeenth centuries hit a magnificent windfall which set them up in business by demonstrating that the game of wealth-getting was both interesting and profitable. For four hundred years, to paraphrase Bernard DeVoto, "men stumbled over fortunes looking for cows." Free homesteads in Kansas, free gold claims in California, and free grass on the Great Plains are examples of windfalls coming at the tag end of the frontier period, windfalls which come no more. In the larger sense the Great Frontier was a windfall for Europe.

There is an unpleasant logic inherent in the frontier boom hypothesis of modern history. We come to it with the reluctance that men always have when they come to the end of a boom. They look back on the grand opportunities they had, they remember the excitement and adventure of it, they tot up their accounts and hope for another chance. Western civilization today stands facing a closed frontier, and in this sense it faces a unique situation in modern times.

If we grant the boom, we must concede that the institutions we have, such as democracy and capitalism, were boomborn; we must also admit that the individual, this cherished darling of modern history, attained his glory in an abnormal period when there was enough room to give him freedom and enough wealth to give him independence. The future of the individual, of democracy and capitalism, and of many other modern institutions are deeply involved in this logic, and the lights are burning late in the capitals of the Western world where grave men are trying to determine what that future will be.

Meantime less thoughtful people speak of new frontiers, though nothing comparable to the Great Frontier has yet been found. The business man sees a business frontier in the customers he has not yet reached; the missionary sees a religious frontier among the souls he has not yet saved; the social worker sees a human frontier among the suffering people whose woes he has not yet alleviated; the educator of a sort sees the ignorance he is trying to dispel as a frontier to be taken; and the scientists permit us to believe that they are uncovering the real thing in a scientific frontier. But as yet no Columbus has come in from these voyages and announced: "Gentlemen, there is your frontier!" The best they do is to say that it is out beyond, that if you work hard enough and have faith enough, and put in a little money, you will surely find it. If you watch these peddlers of substitute frontiers, you will find that nearly every one wants you to buy something, give something, or believe in something. They want you to be a frontier for them. Unlike Columbus, they bring no continents and no oceans, no gold or silver or grass or forest to you.

I should like to make it clear that mankind is really searching for a new frontier which we once had and did not prize, and the longer we had it, the less we valued it; but now that we have lost it, we have a great pain in the heart, and we are always trying to get it back again. It seems to me that historians and all thoughtful persons are bound by their obligation to say that there is no new frontier in sight comparable in magnitude or importance to the one that is lost. They should point out the diversity and heterogeneity, not to say the absurdity, of so-called new frontiers. They are all fallacies, these new frontiers, and they are pernicious in proportion to their plausibility and respectability. The scientists themselves should join in disabusing the public as to what science can be expected to do. It can do much, but, to paraphrase Isaiah Bowman, it is not likely soon to find a new world or make the one we have much bigger than it is. If the frontier is gone, we should have the courage and honesty to recognize the fact, cease to cry for what we have lost, and devote our energy to finding the solutions to the problems now facing a frontierless society. And when the age we now call modern is modern no longer, and requires a new name, we may appropriately call it the Age of the Frontier, and leave it to its place in history.

Stanley Elkins and Eric McKitrick:

A MEANING FOR TURNER'S FRONTIER, DEMOCRACY IN THE OLD NORTHWEST

THOUGH conviction now burns so low, it remains to be noted that even the unkindest of Turner's critics have conceded, with a kind of bedeviled monotony, that *some* relation most likely does exist between our history and our frontier. The fact thus stands that, in this direction at least, no advance has yet been made beyond Turner's own dazzling abstraction. The problem is still there, its vitality unextinguished. It is no further resolved than ever.

If we examine with suspicion the body of critical work, we discover an interesting paradox. Turner and his teachings have been approached with deadly seriousness on their own terms — no other — and handled with what turns out to be *textual* criticism: a method which is illuminating but whose value for the analysis and correction of theoretical material is acutely limited.[1] The result has been to demonstrate the absurdities of Turner's internal logic — which is an undoubted contribution to perspective. Yet it should still be recognized that no concrete attempt to restate Turner's idea has ever actually been undertaken. Now might there not, after all, be a way of rescuing Turner? Is it possible to ask the great question itself in a form permitting a concrete answer?

Turner's critics may be allowed the most sweeping of concessions. Nearly everything[2] could be sacrificed — everything, that is, except the one thing that matters: the development of political democracy as a habit and the American as a unique political creature. This was the supreme fact which overwhelmed Tocqueville in the 1830s; every American still knows in his heart that the frontier had something to do with it. "What?" is, of course, the crucial question. It has always been difficult to ask it, if only be-

[1] The "textual" approach has been used with more success in the analysis of modern poetry and is the principal tool of the "New Criticism." There are indications, however, that even here the method's shortcomings are beginning to be felt. See "The New Criticism," a forum discussion by William Barrett, Kenneth Burke, Malcolm Cowley, Robert Gorham Davis, Allen Tate, and Hiram Haydn, *American Scholar*, XX, 86–104, 218–31 (Jan.-Apr. 1951).

[2] This would involve principally the claim for institutional "novelty" (which puts an extra burden on the theory) and the "safety valve" (which isn't necessary). For that matter, although the frontier assuredly had little to say to the "underprivileged," its *real* "safety valve" aspect is all too seldom stressed. To the part-time real estate operator, whether tobacco planter of the early Tidewater or wheat farmer of the pre-World War Middle Border, the frontier as a safety valve against agricultural bankruptcy has always made perfect sense.

From Stanley Elkins and Eric McKitrick, "A Meaning for Turner's Frontier, Part I: Democracy in the Old Northwest," *Political Science Quarterly*, Vol. LXIX (September, 1954), 323–339. Reprinted by permission.

cause it has never seemed very important to discover a working, functional definition of "political democracy." "Democracy" is alluded to, invoked, celebrated, its collapse predicted daily. Democracy, in our traditions, has rich connections with the yeoman farmer (involving, as it were, "grass roots" and freedom from the urban banker); it is at once individualistic and coöperative, equalitarian and fraternal; hand in hand with stout self-reliance goes the civic exercise of universal suffrage. For most of our daily purposes democracy is a synonym for all that is virtuous in our social traditions and on the public scene.

Yet it still appears that we need a *working* definition of political democracy. It should in some way account for concepts central to most traditional notions, but it should also be functional, in the sense that its terms may be tested. Its focus should undoubtedly be upon participation — participation by large numbers of people in decisions which affect their lives. But it should be real, not ceremonial, participation. The extent of the suffrage would not be its most dependable measure, any more than the casting of one man's vote is the quickest way of influencing a political decision. Awareness of the community's affairs should have something to do with it, but only to the extent that individuals themselves feel capable of interfering in those affairs. Would this be to the community's best interest? Often, but not always; yet here we are not required to think of democracy as a community virtue. Some have, indeed, called it a national vice.

Suppose that political democracy be regarded as a manipulative attitude toward government, shared by large numbers of people. Let it be thought of as a wide participation in public affairs, a diffusion of leadership, a widespread

sense of personal competence to make a difference. Under what conditions have such things typically occurred? When have the energies of the people been most engaged? What pushes a man into public activity? It appears that nothing accomplishes this more quickly than the formation of a settlement.

Our national experience, indeed, furnishes us much material for a hypothesis. Political democracy evolves most quickly during the initial stages of setting up a new community; it is seen most dramatically while the process of organization and the solving of basic problems are still crucial; it is observed to best advantage when this flow of basic problems is met by a homogeneous population. Now "homogeneity" should here involve two parallel sorts of facts: not only a similar level of social and economic status and aspirations among the people, but most particularly a lack of, or failure of, a traditional, ready-made structure of leadership in the community. A simple test of the effectiveness of structured leadership is its ability to command acceptance and respect.[3]

With a heavy flow of community problems, in short, and without such a structure of natural leadership, democracy presents itself much less as a bright possibility than as a brutal necessity. The very incomprehensibility of alternatives has always made it most unlikely that an American should see this. But Tocque-

---

[3] "Not only is leadership limited objectively by given patterns of authority but the will to lead of the leader is vitiated if what he stands for cannot command a following. . . . [The leader's] effectiveness in no small measure derives from how much loyalty he can count upon." Jeremiah F. Wolpert, "Toward a Sociology of Authority," in Alvin W. Gouldner, ed., *Studies in Leadership* (New York, 1950), p. 681. This is the point made by Guglielmo Ferrero in his discussion of "legitimacy"; see *The Principles of Power*, trans. by Theodore Jaeckel (New York, 1942), p. 23.

ville saw it instantly. "In aristocratic societies," he wrote, "men do not need to combine in order to act, because they are strongly held together."

. . . Among democratic nations, on the contrary, all the citizens are independent and feeble; they can hardly do anything by themselves and none of them can oblige his fellow men to lend him their assistance. They all, therefore, fall into a state of incapacity, if they do not learn voluntarily to help each other.[4]

Before turning to history for a trial of this so simple yet interesting idea, let us set it in yet another dimension by examining a series of extremely important findings in contemporary sociology. Robert K. Merton has conducted a study, whose results are soon to be made public, of social behavior in public housing communities.[5] A theory of political democracy which would meet all our criteria may be derived from Mr. Merton's work; there is little that we shall say from a historical viewpoint which has not already, in a present-day setting, been thoroughly documented by him.

He and his associates have observed two public housing projects, one being designated as "Craftown" and the other as "Hilltown." Craftown, located in southern New Jersey, administered by the Federal Public Housing Authority, and set up originally to house warworkers, was much the more active and interesting of the two. The key to the activity there was a "time of troubles" in the initial stages of the community's exist-

[4] *Democracy in America* (Oxford Galaxy Ed., New York, 1946), p. 320.

[5] The study's working title is *Patterns of Social Life: Explorations in the Sociology of Housing*, by Robert K. Merton, Patricia S. West, and Marie Jahoda. We are greatly indebted to Mr. Merton for his generosity in allowing us to examine the material in manuscript.

ence. The people who settled in Craftown ("homogeneous" in the sense that a majority were employed in nearby shipyards and defense plants) were immediately faced by a staggering series of problems of a fundamental sort, affecting the entire community. These bore on law and order, government, public health, housing, education, religion, municipal services, transportation, and markets. Slovenly construction had resulted in leaky roofs, flooded cellars, and warped floors. There were no schools, no churches, no electricity, no community hall, no grocery stores. Bus service was irregular and the nearest depot was a mile away. There were no hard-surfaced roads or sidewalks and much of the area was flooded during the rainy season. There was a wave of vandalism and no organization for its suppression. There was an epidemic of poliomyelitis. There were no municipal services of any kind; the environing township did not want to assume the cost of such services and by legislative action Craftown was gerrymandered into an independent township — which meant that it had to set up its own institutions for government and for the maintenance of law and order.

Craftown did have a ready-made structure, as it were, of leadership; its affairs were under the administration of a federal bureau, the Federal Public Housing Authority, and handled by a resident manager and staff. Under stable conditions such a structure would have been adequate for most of the community's basic concerns. Yet the problems in Craftown were so overwhelming, so immediate, so pressing, that the residents could not afford to wait upon the government for action. They were therefore forced to behave in that same pattern which so fascinated Tocqueville: they were driven to "the forming of associations." Mass meetings, committees and subcommittees were organized, a township board was set up, officials of great variety were elected; a volunteer police force, fire department and local court were established, with residents serving as constables, firemen and judges. A coöperative store soon came into existence. An ambulance squad, a nursery and child care center, and a great variety of organizations devoted to community needs made their appearance during this critical period. Pressures brought upon the bus company and the government agencies resulted in the improvement of transportation, the paving of streets, repair of houses, drainage of swamps, and the erection of buildings for education, worship and other functions of the community.

This experience resulted in an extraordinary level of public participation by people who for the most part had never had previous political experience; and it produced a political life charged with the utmost energy. Many jobs were created by the crisis — by the flow of problems — and they had to be handled by someone; many rôles were created, someone had to fill them. The key was necessity. Persons who had previously never needed to be concerned with politics[6] now found themselves developing a familiarity with institutions, acquiring a sense of personal competence to manipulate them, to make things happen, to make a difference. Thus the coin of necessity had its other side: there were compensations for the individual. With many offices to be filled, large numbers of people found them-

selves contending for them; the prestige connected with officeholding, the sense of energy and power involved in decision-making, became for the first time a possibility, a reality, an exploitable form of self-expression.[7]

Now Hilltown, in contrast to Craftown, may be regarded as something of a control case. Many factors present in Craftown were present here — but a crucial one was missing. Hilltown, like Craftown, was a public housing project in an industrial area; it too was managed by the Federal Public Housing Authority; its population was likewise characterized by "homogeneity" — insofar as that involved a similar level of social and economic status among the residents. What Hilltown did not experience was a "time of troubles." Unlike Craftown, it was well planned and operated, it was not faced with a failure of municipal services, it was not confronted by lack of transportation, stores, electricity, or facilities for education and religion. The residents, to be sure, had their individual problems — occasional badly fitting doors and the like — but they were not of a community nature, not of a sort that made community organization seem indispensable. Widespread public participation in community affairs was never needed there, and it never took place. Sporadic efforts toward the establishment of a council, the election of officers, and the setting up of community activities aroused little interest and met with failure. The orig-

---

[6] Mr. Merton offers various graphs and tables to establish this. In one of them, 88 per cent of the early comers were found to be more highly active in Craftown organizations than in their former communities; only 8 per cent had had the same degree of participation in both communities.

[7] Two other communities, each of which underwent a similar experience in similar circumstances, were Park Forest, Illinois, and Shanks Village, New York, described in William H. Whyte, Jr., "The Future, c/o Park Forest," *Fortune*, June 1953, pp. 126–31, 186–96; and Bernard Horn, "Collegetown: A Study of Transient Student Veteran Families in a Temporary Housing Community" (unpub. M.A. thesis, Columbia University, 1948).

inal structure of leadership — the federal agency and its local office — proved quite adequate for the handling of Hilltown's concerns, it was never seriously challenged, and it required no supplementation by resident activity.[8] "Democracy," in short, was unnecessary there.

One more reference to the Craftown episode should be made, in order to note two interesting subsidiary consequences of this problem-solving experience, this wide participation, this sense of individual competence spread among such great numbers. One was a close supervision of the officialdom which the Craftowners themselves had created — and a lesser degree of respect for it[9] than had apparently been the case in their previous communities. The other was a body of shared "traditions," with a common vocabulary, rich with meaning, whereby the experience might be relived and reshared. Although the level of activity was never as high in later times as it was in the beginning — the problems by then had been solved — the intensity of the "time of troubles" served to link the "pioneers" and the later-comers together by a kind of a verbal bond. Talking about it was important: once this experience had

been undergone, it was not lost. In such a usable fund of tradition, resources for meeting a new crisis, should one appear, would remain always available.[10]

How might such a contemporary model square with the pioneer frontier? No sorcery of forest or prairie could materialize the democrat, yet it should be safe to guess that the periods of wholesale migration to the West forced a setting in which such an experience as that just outlined had to be enacted a thousand times over: an experience crucial in the careers of millions of Americans. Frederick Jackson Turner has stated the undeniable fact—that an organic connection exists between American democracy and the American frontier. The insight is his. But Turner never offered a conceptual framework by which it might be tested. We are proposing such a model; it involves the establishment of new communities. Its variables are a period of problem-solving and a homogeneous population whose key factor is the lack of a structure of leadership. We shall test these terms in various ways by the examination of three frontiers, each of which should illustrate a special dimension of the argument. They are the Old

---

[8] Thus "homogeneity" — in the total sense which we have given that concept — did not exist in Hilltown. There was a clear distinction — to extend the analogy — between "the rulers and the ruled."

[9] These facts seem to go together. An illuminating Craftown anecdote concerns a woman who was fined $5 by one of the locally elected judges for letting her dog run loose. "Well, that's just like working men," she declared. "A rich man wouldn't be so interested in money. . . . I don't think any working man should mix in politics. I think a man that has money is better able to rule." It is at the same time quite possible to imagine the same woman making *this* statement (also recorded at Craftown): "I never voted in the city for mayor or things like that. I just didn't have the interest. In the city they get in anyhow and there's nothing you can do about it. Here they're more connected with people."

[10] Mr. Merton points out that this phenomenon was taken as a concrete cultural fact by Malinowski, who called it "phatic communion." "Each utterance is an act serving the direct aim of binding hearer to speaker by a tie of some social sentiment or other . . . language appears to us in this function not as an instrument of reflection but as a mode of action." Bronislaw Malinowski, in C. K. Ogden and I. A. Richards, *The Meaning of Meaning* (New York, 1923), pp. 478–79. The connection between this kind of thing and the folklore of democracy is seldom appreciated: consider, for example, the typical American reaction to disaster — the ease with which the traditions of the frontier are converted into spontaneous organizational techniques for coping with the emergency. The community response to the tornado which struck Flint, Michigan, in 1953 provides a perfect case in point; examples like it are numberless.

Northwest, the Southwest frontier of Alabama and Mississippi, and the Puritan frontier of Massachusetts Bay.

"The frontier," to Turner and his followers, as well as to most others, seemed almost automatically to mean the Old Northwest — the "valley of democracy" — whose settlement took place during the first third of the nineteenth century. To discover why the connection should be made so naturally, let us select this region, with its key states Ohio, Indiana and Illinois, as the first frontier to be observed.

The chronicles of these states abound with reminiscences of the pioneer; close upon them in the county histories came haphazard statistics which proudly mark progress from howling wilderness to fat countryside and prosperous burgs. Between these points come many a crisis, many a relished success. We should consider not the solitary drifters, the Daniel Boones, but the thousand isolated communities each of which in its own way must have undergone its "time of troubles." There, the basic problems of organization were intimately connected with matters of life and death. They were problems to be met only by the united forces of the community. Think of the basic question of housing itself, and how its solution was elevated by necessity, throughout the Old Northwest, to the status of institution and legend: the cabin-raising.[11] The clearing of the forest

and the manner in which this was accomplished gave an idiom to our politics: the logrolling.[12] Defense against the Indians required that the experience of the Marietta settlers, forced to raise their own militia in the 1790s, be repeated elsewhere many times over at least until after the War of 1812.[13] And there was the question of law and order: the traveler Elias Fordham, stopping one night in 1818 at a cabin near Paoli, Indiana, found himself in the midst of preparations by the citizenry for apprehending a gang of brigands. How often must such a scene — the formation of *ad hoc* constabularies, the administration of emergency justice — have been enacted in those days?[14]

Close behind such supreme needs came that of educating the young, which claimed an early order of concern throughout the Northwest. Traveling instructors were often employed to go from house to house; later, when the children

[11] "When the time comes, and the forces collect together, a captain is appointed, and the men divide into proper sections, and [are] assigned to their several duties." Henry B. Curtis, "Pioneer Days in Central Ohio," *O. State Arch. and Hist. Pubs.*, I, 245 (1887). Almost any state or county history or pioneer memoir will refer to or describe this familiar social function; see, e.g., William T. Utter, *The Frontier State* (Columbus, 1942), pp. 138, 139–41; W. C. Howells, *Recollections of Life in Ohio* (Cincinnati, 1895), pp. 144–51; etc., etc.

[12] There is a vivid contemporary description of a combined logrolling and political rally in Baynard Rush Hall, *The New Purchase*, James A. Woodburn, ed. (Princeton, 1916), pp. 202–205. See also Logan Esarey, *History of Indiana* (Indianapolis, 1915), pp. 421, 425–26.

[13] Beverly W. Bond, Jr., *The Civilization of the Old Northwest* (New York, 1934), pp. 249, 268, 351, 357. "The shrill whistle of the fife and the beat of the drum, calling to arms for the defense of their countrymen, was answered by many a gray-haired sire and many a youthful pioneer." H. W. Chadwick, comp., *Early History of Jackson County* (Brownstown, Ind., 1943), p. 14. The War of 1812 in the Northwest, particularly in Ohio, had as much or more to do with hostile Indians as with the British, and defense was typically handled by the raising of local militia. See "Ohio and the War of 1812," ch. iv in Utter, *op. cit.*, pp. 88–119.

[14] Elias P. Fordham, *Personal Narrative*, ed. by Frederic Ogg (Cleveland, 1906), pp. 154–55; Hall, *op. cit.*, p. 196; Charles Francis Ingals, "A Pioneer in Lee County, Illionis," ed. by Lydia Colby, *Ill. State Hist. Soc. Jour.*, XXVI, 281 (Oct. 1933).

could pass through the forest without danger, they might gather for a time at one of the settlers' houses until community labor could be assembled to put up a school.[15] The demand for religion was little less urgent; first came the circuit rider to a house or barn designated for worship; denominational differences might then have to be submerged in the erection of a common chapel until each sect could build its own meeting house.[16] Even problems of public health, with no hospitals and few doctors, had to be solved occasionally under heroic circumstances. When cholera struck Jacksonville, Illinois, in 1833, the cabinetmaker John Henry boarded thirteen persons at his house for three weeks, supervised a crew of assistants in the building of coffins for each of the fifty-five dead, personally visited each house of sickness, took fifty-three corpses to the burying ground, and, assisted by two farmers, a blacksmith, a shoemaker, a brickmaker

and a carpenter, dug the graves and interred the dead — a series of functions quite above the line of normal business.[17]

Now as these communities toiled through the process of stabilizing their affairs, what effect must such an experience have had upon the individuals themselves, exposed as they were to the sudden necessity of making great numbers of basic and vital decisions, private and public? With thousands of ambitious men, predominantly young men[18] looking for careers, pouring into vast unsettled tracts, setting up new communities, and being met with all the complex hazards of such an adventure, the scope and variety of new political experience was surely tremendous. A staggering number of public rôles was thrust forward during such an enterprise, far too many to wait upon the appearance of seasoned leaders. With the organization of each wilderness county and pioneer township, the roster of offices to be filled and operated was naturally a perfect blank (how long had it been since this was so in Philadelphia?); somebody, willing or unwilling, must be found to fill each one.

Whether farmers, lawyers, merchants, artisans, or even men of means, the "leading citizens" in county after county were

---

[15] "As soon as conditions were favorable the pioneers of the neighborhood constructed a rude cabin schoolhouse. . . . There was no school revenue to be distributed, so each voter himself had to play the part of the builder. The neighbors divided themselves into choppers, hewers, carpenters, and masons. Those who found it impossible to report for duty might pay an equivalent in nails, boards, or other materials. The man who neither worked nor paid was fined thirty-seven and one-half cents a day." William F. Vogel, "Home Life in Early Indiana," *Ind. Mag. of Hist.*, X, 297 (Sept. 1914).

[16] The "interfaith chapel" was invariably the early solution to this problem (there was one in Craftown, also in Park Forest and Shanks Village). "The first church . . . was free to all denominations, and here, for miles and miles came the pioneer and family on the Sabbath day to worship God." Chadwick, *op. cit.*, p. 35. See also Vogel, *loc. cit.*, p. 291; Morris Birkbeck, *Letters from Illinois* (London, 1818), p. 23; John D. Barnhardt, Jr., "The Rise of the Methodist Episcopal Church in Illinois from the Beginning to the Year 1832," *Ill. State Hist. Soc. Jour.*, XII, 149–217 (July 1919).

[17] C. H. Rammelkamp, ed., "The Memoirs of John Henry: A Pioneer of Morgan County," *Ill. State Hist. Soc. Jour.*, XVIII, 55 (Apr. 1925).

[18] In a history of the town of Lancaster, Ohio, which was founded in 1800, there is a longish series of biographical sketches of its "leading pioneers." Twenty-seven of these sketches concern settlers who arrived within the first ten years of the town's existence and who held office, and of these 27, age data are given for 15. For what such a haphazard sample is worth, the average age of this group at the date of the town's founding was twenty-four. C. M. L. Wiseman, *Centennial History of Lancaster* (Lancaster, 1898).

typically men of no previous political experience.[19] For example, there was Morgan County, Illinois. Its first settler was Seymour Kellogg, who brought his wife and seven children from New York State, was made a commissioner at the first election and shortly afterward became justice of the peace. Murray Mc-Connel, who read law on his farm at odd hours and became Jacksonville's first lawyer, was forthwith sent to the legislature (though unwillingly) and later served the community in various other capacities. Jacksonville's first cabinet-maker, the aforementioned John Henry (scarcely literate), was drawn into politics immediately, and before his career was over had been an assemblyman, state senator and member of Congress, not to say superintendent of the local insane asylum and patron of learning to the Female Academy. The first printer there was Josiah Lucas, who had arrived from Maryland ("without friends") and established a paper with local support. Championing Henry Clay, he was shortly in a maelstrom of politics, and the experience thus gained netted him a postmastership to the House of Representatives and "many offices both civil and military," culminating in a minister's post in Europe.[20] Variations on this typical pat-

tern are to be found in county after county in the Old Northwest.[21]

What we exhibit here are the elements of a simple syllogism; the first settlers anywhere, no matter who they were or how scanty their prior political experience, were the men who had to be the first officeholders. This meant that the pioneers, in the very process of establishing and organizing their settlements, were faced with a burden of decision-making disproportionate to that exacted of the later-comers. The political lore, the manipulative skills, which must have been acquired in that process should somehow be kept in the foreground when judging the ferocious vitality, the extravagant energy, of early political life in the Old Northwest.

Inasmuch as many new political rôles were being created by the needs of this new society, both necessity and opportunities for political careers might more and more be seen reflected in the long lists of candidates and high level of participation. In Hamilton County, Ohio, there was an election of delegates to the constitutional convention of 1802, and for ten openings there were ninety-four candidates — twenty-six of them receiving from 121 to 1,635 votes apiece.[22] The

---

[19] The county histories make every effort to secure the immortality of their leading citizens by reciting as many of their accomplishments as are known. Thus if the biographical sketches make no mention of public office held elsewhere, it should be safe to assume that at least in most of the cases their civic careers began in the new settlement.

[20] Frank S. Heinl, "The First Settlers in Morgan County," *Ill. State Hist. Soc. Jour.*, XVIII, 76–87 (Apr. 1925); Rammelkamp, *loc. cit.*, pp. 39–40 and *passim;* George Murray McConnel, "Some Reminiscences of My Father, Murray McConnel," *Ill. State Hist. Soc. Jour.*, XVIII, 89–100 (Apr. 1925).

[21] The seemingly fabulous Wesley Park — who was the first settler at Auburn, Indiana, and DeKalb County's first sheriff, road commissioner, road supervisor, jail commissioner, and clerk of the first county board — was actually a figure quite typical. We see blacksmith-judges and carpenter-sheriffs everywhere. See S. W. Widney, "Pioneer Sketches of DeKalb County," *Ind. Mag. of Hist.*, XXV, 116, 125–26, 128 (June 1929). "Few of the officials prior to 1950 [in Parke County, Indiana] were men of education. For years it was the custom to elect a coroner from among the stalwart blacksmiths. . . ." Maurice Murphy, "Some Features of the History of Parke County," *Ind. Mag. of Hist.*, XII, 151 (June 1916).

[22] Bond, *op. cit.*, pp. 102, 124.

personal canvass, the practice of hawking one's political appeal from door to door, not generally assumed to have entered American politics until the Jacksonian era, was familiar in the Northwest well before 1824. A cabin-dweller's effusion in the *Illinois Intelligencer* of July 1, 1818, describes how hosts of candidates, at the approach of an election, would descend upon him with whisky, trinkets for the children, compliments, and grand promises.

> But what most rarely does my good wife please,
> Is that the snot nos'd baby gets a buss![23]

"And every body," wrote Baynard Rush Hall of Indiana's New Purchase, "expected at some time to be a candidate for something; or that his uncle would be; or his cousin, or his cousin's wife's cousin's friend would be; so that every body and every body's relations, and every body's relations' friends, were for ever electioneering." Even boys verging on manhood were "feared, petted, courted and cajoled."[24] Such arts of cajolery could be appropriate and necessary only to a society in which officials were watched far more closely and respected far less than was the magistrate of Boston or the justice of the peace in Fairfax County, Virginia. Hall, an Easterner of refinement, reflected with deep distaste that if "eternal vigilance" were the price of liberty it was well paid in the New Purchase, the "sovereign people" there being "the most uncompromising

task masters": "Our officers all, from Governor down to a deputy constable's deputy and fence-viewer's clerk's first assistant, were in the direct gift of the people. We even elected magistrates, clerks of court, and the judges presiding and associate!"[25]

Thus the extraordinary animation with which the people of Craftown flung themselves into political activity may be seen richly paralleled in the life of the Old Northwest. Every militia muster, every cabin-raising, scow-launching, shooting match, and logrolling was in itself a political assembly where leading figures of the neighborhood made speeches, read certificates, and contended for votes. Sometimes at logrollings rival candidates would take charge of opposing sections of workers, fitness for office having much to do with whose group disposed of its logs first. The enterprising farmer understood, it is said, that this political energy could be exploited at its height about a month before election time, and tried to schedule his logrolling accordingly.[26]

Our concept of political democracy, it may be remembered, involved a homogeneous population. Can it be asserted that these early Northwest communities were characterized by such a population? There is striking evidence that both attributes of "homogeneity" — a similar level of aspiration and status, and conditions rendering impossible a prior structure of leadership — were widely present here, just as they were in Craftown. A leading symptom of this may be found in

---

[23] Quoted in Solon J. Buck, *Illinois in 1818* (Springfield, 1917), p. 260. Consider again the power of "phatic communion": in the 1952 presidential election the governor of that same great state of Illinois might have been seen blandly kissing babies.

[24] Hall, *New Purchase*, p. 178.

[25] *Ibid.*, pp. 200–201, 177.

[26] Vogel, *loc. cit.*, p. 309. "Our candidates certainly sweat for their expected honours," Hall remarks. ". . . Nay, a very few hundreds of rival and zealous candidates would, in a year or so, if judiciously driven under proper task masters, clear a considerable territory." *Op. cit.*, p. 205.

the land arrangements. Beverly Bond has made calculations, based on lists of lands advertised for delinquent taxes, as to typical holdings in the Northwest about 1812, and concludes that the "average farm" at that time was probably less than 250 acres.[27] Though such tentative statistics are embarrassing in themselves, the limiting conditions which make them plausible are clear enough — uniform conditions not only permitting but forcing a reduced scale of holdings. Much has been made of large engrossments of land by speculators in the Northwest Territory, yet before the admission of Ohio in 1803, and many years before that of Indiana and Illinois, it was apparent to all that the day of the great land magnate was at an end. His operations were doomed by the very techniques of settlement and by the measures taken by the settlers themselves to thwart his designs.

Despite large quantities of government land on the market, much of which was bought by speculators, the attraction of choice locations led regularly to settlement in advance of purchase — squatting, in short — especially when sales were delayed, as they often were. Thousands of such petty *faits accomplis* all over the Northwest frontier could hardly be reversed,[28] no matter how powerful the petitioners, and the terms of sale, re-

flected in a series of land laws ever more generous,[29] were but one indication of such a state of things. An even more formidable token of doom to the great absentee holder was revealed in the tax rates levied on unimproved land by the early legislatures. While all these future states were still under one territorial assembly, that body at its first session passed a law taxing three grades of land — a law which was only the first of several, each more severe than its predecessor, consecrated to the mission of breaking up large unimproved tracts held by nonresidents. Increasing powers were given to local sheriffs presiding over the sales of delinquent holdings.[30] This meant that in practice the large speculator, forced as he was to pay cash for these tracts, must effect relatively quick turnovers in a buyer's market: there was really plenty of land to be had and the costs of holding it for a rise were becoming higher year by year.[31] For the rest, with labor costs uniformly high and with a population whose average resources, either in land or in liquid wealth, must initially be moderate, the great farm on the Southern model could never be a widespread reality. What this particularly indicates is that a land-holding élite — with all the traditional functions, social and political, that such an élite would certainly exercise — was rendered quite out of the question. The leadership of *this* society would have to be recruited on manifestly different terms.

[27] *Civilization of the Old Northwest*, pp. 331–32.

[28] Buck, *op. cit.*, pp. 47, 54–55. "The situation was so serious that the matter was taken up with the secretary of state, and the president issued a proclamation directing that after a certain day in March, 1816, all squatters on the public lands should be removed. Against the execution of this proclamation, Benjamin Stephenson, the delegate from Illinois territory, protested vigorously. . . . The marshal of the Illinois territory actually made preparations to remove the intruders; but the secretary of the treasury wrote him on May 11, 1816, recommending 'a prudent and conciliatory course'; and nothing seems to have been accomplished." *Ibid.*, p. 54.

[29] Notably the Congressional legislation of 1796, 1800 and 1804.

[30] Bond, *op. cit.*, pp. 337–38.

[31] A special situation in Illinois added to the difficulty of amassing large absentee holdings; actual sales of public land could not begin there until 1814 owing to the perplexity of the French claims, and the result was a growing population of squatters and slim pickings for speculators. Buck, *op. cit.*, p. 44.

Who was it, then, that organized the pressure for these land acts; who goaded the federal Congress into passing them; who connived in the legislature; who wrote the tax laws? Who indeed but the frontier politician who kissed the "snot nos'd baby" in that lonely cabin? He well understood how his majorities depended upon the zeal with which he and his friends could manipulate the government on their constituents' behalf. Their problems were concrete; the guaranteeing of preëmption rights was an urgency of the topmost order; this was the primary stimulus which forced the tax laws, the universal suffrage clauses in the state constitutions, and the Congressional land legislation. The "sovereign people" of the Old Northwest was a "most uncompromising task master" to its servants. Symbolic of the future was the case of William Henry Harrison, to whom fell the unhappy office of mediating, so to speak, between "the people" and the Northwest's greatest land speculator, John Cleves Symmes. Harrison, as territorial delegate to Congress, was successful in bringing about the Land Act of 1800 in the interests of the settlers but a dismal failure in his efforts to get justice for Symmes, his father-in-law, whose vast holdings in Ohio were crumbling away in an avalanche of claims and judgments. The unfortunate Symmes was no match for a thousand ruthless frontier manipulators.[32] The democracy of the Northwest would be that of the squatter, the frontier business man, and, no doubt, that of the *small* speculator.

Granted that a structure of *landed* political leadership was impossible, might not a different species of élite appear, say an élite of lawyers? It is true that admission to the bar in the early days was a virtual guarantee of political advancement. But the stability of any such structure must be certified by some recognized assurance of self-perpetuation. The very recruitment patterns, the conditions under which political preferment had to be gained and held in the Northwest, should make us think twice before considering the great majority of lawyers in politics there as constituting such a structure. Every lawyer was literally on his own. It was the desperate need for wits and talent on the frontier that gave him his chance, a chance renewed by the community as long as he continued to deliver. Here the rôles of patron and client are reversed; it is difficult for a "ruling class" to establish and guarantee tenure under such conditions. Murray McConnel, the self-made lawyer of Jacksonville, was once warned that his politically ambitious young clerk — Stephen Douglas — was using him as a steppingstone. "No matter," he replied, "his ambition will probably prove of more worth to the nation than all our modesty."[33] This was about the only kind of laying on of hands possible in the Northwest: the embodiment of success, of frontier virtue, was the self-made man.

What we have done so far is to discover a kind of "primitive" level of the

[32] Symmes had sold, in advance, a number of tracts outside his 1792 patent, expecting to take them up at 66⅔ cents an acre. Subsequently the price rose to $2.00, on which Symmes could not possibly make good. An original contract for 1,000,000 acres had been partly paid for in Continental certificates, and the patent of 1792 gave him title to those lands for which he had paid. Neither his influence nor that of Harrison was ever able to guarantee the entire claim of 1,000,-000 acres. Meanwhile the Scioto Company had completely collapsed, and the representations of the Illinois and Wabash companies met with even less success than did those of Symmes.

[33] McConnel, *loc. cit.*, p. 95.

frontier experience, a level at which a vast flow of problems forced a high degree of participation in the making of decisions, an acute pitch of political awareness among the settlers. The traditions of the pioneers remind us that this experience was not lost. An egalitarian tone was set, and ceremonial observances by which the experience was reinvoked and reshared made their way into the social habits of the people. Stephen Douglas, for one, understood its obligations, and by stopping at Geneva on one of his county canvasses to assist at a logrolling he was performing a symbolic act.[34]*

[34] Heinl, *loc. cit.*, p. 84. See also *supra*, note 15.

* The Elkins-McKitrick modification of the Turner hypothesis actually contains two phases, though space permits us to reproduce only one of them. The second part of their argument anticipates the question of why the political life of one frontier should have been more "democratic" than that of another, together with the question of what may have been the mechanism for perpetuating a "democratic" situation once the "problem-solving" experience was over and the community's basic arrangements stabilized. Their answer is found in the petty capitalism of the small town, seen most strikingly in the development of the Old Northwest, where towns of 200 or more population existed in about six times the ratio per capita as could be found in the essentially rural frontier of Alabama and Mississippi. The variety of civic needs experienced in an expanding small-business community, the authors argue, keeps the public life of such a community dynamic and open. It is this fact, they feel, that is most neglected in the folklore of American democracy: the kinship, as it were, between the democrat-pioneer and the democrat-promoter. — Ed.

Suggestions for Additional Reading

The student who wishes to read more of Turner may do so in two books of his essays: *The Frontier in American History* (New York, 1920) and *The Significance of Sections in American History* (New York, 1932). An essay entitled "Social Forces in American History" in the former book will be found especially valuable for an understanding of his frontier thesis. Frederic L. Paxson has contributed a laudatory restatement of Turner's thesis in "A Generation of the Frontier Hypothesis: 1893–1932," *Pacific Historical Review*, 2 (1933), 34–51. Sympathetic interpretations of Turner and his methods will be found in Fulmer Mood, "The Development of Frederick Jackson Turner as a Historical Thinker," *Publications of the Colonial Society of Massachusetts*, 34 (1943), 283–352, and Merle E. Curti, "The Section and the Frontier in American History: The Methodological Concepts of Frederick Jackson Turner," in *Methods in Social Science*, edited by Stuart A. Rice (Chicago, 1931), pp. 353–367. Also on Turner's method but somewhat more critical is James C. Malin, "The Turner-Mackinder Space Concept of History," *Essays on Historiography* (Lawrence, Kansas, 1946), pp. 1–44. An excellent survey of the methods used by American historians with special emphasis on Turner will be found in an essay by John Herman Randall, Jr., and George Haines IV, entitled "Controlling Assumptions in the Practice of American Historians," in *Theory and Practice in Historical Study: A Report of the Committee on Histori-*ography (New York, Social Science Research Council, 1946), pp. 15–52.

No clear understanding of Turner is possible without some appreciation of his great influence as a teacher. Carl Becker, certainly one of the ablest of Turner's students, describes Turner as a teacher in an essay entitled "Frederick Jackson Turner" which appears as Chapter 9 in *American Masters of Social Science*, edited by Howard W. Odum (New York, 1927). It is perhaps as genuine and as eloquent a tribute as has ever been paid by a scholar to his teacher.

For views definitely hostile to the frontier hypothesis other writings by both Wright and Pierson may well be consulted. In an article entitled "American Democracy and the Frontier," *Yale Review*, 20 (1930), 349–365, Wright stresses the importance of Eastern as against frontier influences in the development of our democracy. Pierson subjects Turner's thesis to detailed criticism in "The Frontier and Frontiersmen of Turner's Essay," *Pennsylvania Magazine of History and Biography*, 64 (1940), 449–478. A different critical approach may be found in Murray Kane, "Some Considerations of the Frontier Concept of Frederick Jackson Turner," *Mississippi Valley Historical Review*, 27 (1940–41), 379–400. Kane rebels against Turner as a historian but accepts him as a geographer. A summary statement of critical views will be found in Richard Hofstadter, "Turner and the Frontier Myth," *American Scholar*, XVIII (Oct., 1949), 433–443. Henry Nash Smith's,

Virgin Land, The American West as Symbol and Myth (Cambridge, 1950) provides a literary interpretation. In Chapter XXII he finds fault with the thesis because of its acceptance of the "contradictory ideas of nature and civilization." David M. Potter in his *People of Plenty, Economic Abundance and the American Character* (Chicago, 1954, see especially Chapter VII) emphasizes the role of technology in creating abundance. He accepts part and rejects part of the frontier thesis as developed by Turner and Walter Prescott Webb.

For discussions of the safety-valve theory relating to the frontier, a topic not emphasized in the readings in this volume, see Fred A. Shannon, "A Post Mortem on the Labor-Safety-Valve Theory," *Agricultural History*, (Jan., 1945), 31–37; Carter Goodrich and Sol Davison, "The Wage-Earner in the Westward Movement I," *Political Science Quarterly*, 50 (June, 1935), 161–185, and "The Wage-Earner in the Westward Movement II," *Political Science Quarterly*, 51 (March, 1936), 61–116; and Murray Kane, "Some Considerations on the Safety Valve Doctrine," *Mississippi Valley Historical Review*, 23 (September, 1936), 169–188.

The student who is interested in recent developments of the frontier hypothesis should read further in the authors whose works constitute the last two selections in this volume: Walter Prescott Webb, *The Great Frontier* (Cambridge, Mass., 1952) and Stanley Elkins and Eric McKitrick, "A Meaning for Turner's Frontier," Part I: "Democracy in the Old Northwest" and Part II "The Southwest Frontier and New England," *Political Science Quarterly*, Vol. LXIX (Sept., 1954), 321–353, and (Dec., 1954), 565–602.

Those who wish to delve still more deeply into this subject should consult *The Early Writings of Frederick Jackson Turner* (Madison, 1938). In addition to a careful reproduction of Turner's early writings, this book contains an instructive essay entitled "Turner's Formative Period" by Fulmer Mood and an elaborate Turner bibliography by Everett E. Edwards. A good bibliography on the dispute over the frontier thesis may be found in Ray Allen Billington, *Westward Expansion, A History of the American Frontier* (New York, 1949), pp. 760–762. This book is recommended to the student who wishes to know more of the history of the frontier or who needs bibliographical assistance on the subject. A select list of source documents on the frontier, together with helpful comments, may be found in Fulmer Mood's "The Concept of the Frontier, 1871–1898," in *Agricultural History*, 19 (1945), 24–30.